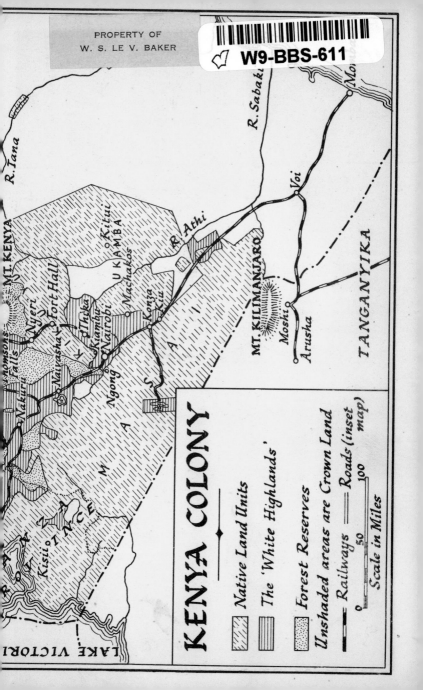

MAU MAU
AND THE KIKUYU

MAU MAU
AND THE KIKUYU

L. S. B. Leakey

METHUEN & CO. LTD., LONDON
36 Essex Street, Strand, W.C.2

To the memory of
my great friend Chief Waruhiu
I dedicate this book

First published December 11th 1952
Reprinted seven times
Reprinted, 1954
1.8
CATALOGUE NO 5448/U

PRINTED IN GREAT BRITAIN

CONTENTS

Endpaper map drawn by
N. S. Hyslop

PREFACE

Some years ago I finished a very detailed study of the customs of the Kikuyu tribe, a book which, when published, will run to some 1,400 pages of print. It was my earnest hope that the publication of that book would help to make the Europeans of Kenya understand a little more about the Kikuyu people and so avoid the many mistakes which, so often, cause misunderstanding and enmity between the two groups.

But publication was delayed, and is delayed, and now the misunderstandings on the part of the European and the distrust on the part of the Kikuyu have reached a point where evil people have been able to bring into existence the present Mau Mau troubles, which I feel sure could have been avoided and need never have happened.

I have written this smaller book in the hope that a brief summary of some of the more important Kikuyu customs, and a discussion of their break-down under the impact of European civilization in the short space of fifty years, may help to make the British understand two things: why and how the Mau Mau has come into being, and also how, when it has been suppressed, things can be improved so that such a state of affairs need never again disturb the peace of the land I love so much—Kenya. As I am better known for my work on the Prehistory of East Africa than as a student of social problems, I had better briefly state why I have felt qualified to write this book.

I was born and bred among the Kikuyu people, where my parents, who were C.M.D. missionaries, lived and worked for so long. I speak the Kikuyu language as well as, if not better than, English. I spent most of my youth with the Kikuyu, I am a member of the Kikuyu age-group called

Mukanda, from which, I regret to say, not a few Mau Mau leaders have sprung. Others of my age-group are strongly anti-Mau Mau. I am also an initiated first-grade elder (*Muthuri wa mburi imwe*) of the tribe and I gave up two and a half years from my work on Prehistory in order to prepare my detailed book on the Kikuyu, working throughout this time with Kikuyu elders and with men of my age-group so as to be sure that all that I wrote down was absolutely correct.

I feel that, perhaps, I know the Kikuyu better than any white man living—I am in so many ways a Kikuyu myself—and that is why I have dared to write this book, hoping and praying that it may help to bring understanding of the problems of the tribe and, in due course, peace to all the people of Kenya.

INTRODUCTION

In September 1952 it became necessary for the Kenya Government to declare a State of Emergency, as a result of the activities of an organization known as Mau Mau. Troops had to be flown out to the Colony, the Police Force had to be strengthened, the Police Reserve had to be mobilized and the Kenya Regiment called into action. Nobody knows how long this State of Emergency will last, or what the future holds in store, before peace and confidence can be restored and the normal life of the Colony be resumed.

Mau Mau is openly anti-White and also anti-Christian. It aims to drive the Europeans and all other foreigners out of the country and intends to use murder, intimidation, and, finally, a general uprising to bring this about. Had it been possible for the Mau Mau organization to remain really secret until the leaders thought the time was ripe for the action which they planned, the consequences might have been very serious indeed.

The plans of the Mau Mau leaders necessitated trying to make nearly every Kikuyu in the country a member, and in order to achieve this end they instituted as a *sine qua non* of membership a ceremony of oath-taking based upon old tribal custom, but which violated ancient custom in many ways. The oath which had to be taken by members was very carefully thought out and so worded that once a person had taken it, even under pressure, there would be little risk of his reporting the facts to the authorities.

In the initial stages of the movement, membership was voluntary, but in the past two years all kinds of pressure has been brought to bear on the members of the Kikuyu tribe to force them to join the Mau Mau. This has not only consisted of threats of physical violence and of damage to property, but of acts of torture and even the murder of people who steadfastly refused to join. As the movement grew and its aims and objects became better known among the masses, opposition began to harden and was led by such men as Chief Waruhiu, Chief Nderi and Mr. Harry Thuku. Mau Mau then showed its hand further and began to plan and carry out the murders of people who opposed it. At the same time, some of the less responsible followers, who had pledged themselves on oath to kill a white man when 'the trumpet sounded', murdered certain Europeans before being given the signal to start doing so by the leaders.

With the declaration of the State of Emergency, Government acted swiftly and competently and a large number of the people who were believed to be the real leaders of Mau Mau were quickly arrested. Prior to this, as a result of the fact that there had been a number of stalwart men and women who, not counting the cost to themselves, had reported on Mau Mau activities to the Police, after having been forced to take the oath against their will, there had been a good many arrests among the lesser members of the organization. Great difficulties had been encountered, however, when these people were brought to trial, for on many occasions the witnesses simply disappeared. They had either been murdered or so intimidated that they would not appear in court to give evidence against their oppressors.

Since the movement has its greatest following among members of the Kikuyu tribe, not only those who live in the Native land units or 'Reserves', as they were formerly called, but also those living in the towns and cities and on European farms, we must clearly try to understand something about this tribe if we are to grasp the reasons why it was possible for unscrupulous leaders to force Mau Mau on the masses.

In the chapters that follow I shall first of all give a summary of some of the more important customs and beliefs of the Kikuyu tribe, as they were before the white man came and until about the time of the outbreak of the First World War. This will form Part I of the book and it will provide the essential background against which Part II can be studied.

In Part II, I shall try to show how the break-down of Kikuyu law, custom, religious beliefs, and training of the young people, and the substitution either of modifications or new ideas has led to a state of affairs in which Mau Mau could operate. I shall also try to show why it is that 'Land' is the rallying cry used by the Mau Mau to win adherents.

I shall also try to explain why the Mau Mau oath is such a potent weapon, and why it is so difficult for people who had taken this oath under pressure to seek to be 'cleansed' from its effect, until Government had shown that it would afford protection to those who did so.

Finally, I shall attempt to outline some of the things that perhaps can be done to prevent a movement like Mau Mau from starting up all over again, once the present situation has been cleared up.

PART ONE

The Kikuyu before the coming of the European

I

THE KIKUYU AND THEIR LAND

The Kikuyu tribe, or, as they call themselves, the Agikuyu, is one of the Bantu-speaking peoples of East Africa and the biggest and most important tribe in Kenya. The Mau Mau terrorist movement which is, at the moment, causing so much trouble, is composed almost entirely of Kikuyu people. In consequence, if we are to understand the underlying causes which made it possible for the movement to come into being and to reach the proportions which it has reached, we must know something of the history and customs of the Kikuyu and, still more, we must understand their relationship over the years with the British Government and the other Europeans who have settled in Kenya.

The Kikuyu traditionally trace their origin to a woman Muumbi, who had as husband and father of her children one Gikuyu. The offspring of Muumbi and Gikuyu are regarded as the founders of the nine Kikuyu clans and each clan is named after one of them. According to tradition the Kikuyu first started as a tribe in the Fort Hall district, the exact point of origin supposedly being at 'Mukuruwe wa Gathanga', marked by a large acacia or *Mukuruwe* tree. As the descendants of Muumbi grew in numbers and multiplied they first of all spread over the area which is now the Fort Hall or Muranga district, felling the forest and carving out fields and gardens for themselves and their children. Tradition relates that the only inhabitants before the spread of the Kikuyu and their occupation of this area were a people of small stature and hideous features known as the Agumba, who 'lived in holes in the ground' into which they disappeared whenever they were frightened.

All over this part of Kikuyu country can be found scattered saucer-shaped depressions from eight to twenty feet in diameter. From excavations that have been made of similar depressions in other parts of Kenya, we know that these holes represent the partially filled-in pits of very late Stone Age and Early Iron Age underground pit dwellings. Similar underground huts are still in use among the Wambulu of Tanganyika Territory (although these are of larger size), and we may, with some degree of certainty, identify the Agumba as a small group of surviving pre-historic peoples who were living as hunters in the forest when the agricultural Kikuyu started to occupy what is now the Fort Hall district some hundreds of years ago.

It is not easy to fix in any certain way the date of the birth of the Kikuyu tribe—the *Ciana cia Muumbi*—but it was probably some seven or eight hundred years ago, for the tribe had increased in numbers to such an extent by the late sixteenth century that they had to find fresh living room. The movement southwards across the Chania River into what is now known as the Kiambu district of Kikuyu land started about that time, as did a movement north-wards into the area now called Nyeri, lying at the foot of Mount Kenya. The expansion northwards into the forested foothills round Mount Kenya was, according to tradition, a slow and simple process of penetration into a zone which had no occupants at all (or at the most a few Agumba), but the movement to the south across the Chania was entirely different and the differences are of vital importance to an understanding of Kikuyu land problems today and of some of the real grievances which underlie the Mau Mau movement.

By Kikuyu law and custom, land occupied and owned by other people cannot be acquired simply by conquest, for if this were done and the previous owner forcibly dis-possessed, the Kikuyu fully believed that the spirits of the owners would make it impossible for the new occupiers to carry out their agricultural activities with any hope of success, or with any hope of the blessing of *Ngai*, the God of the Kikuyu. Now the whole of the forested land lying south of the Chania River and between that river and the Ngong Hills was formerly occupied by a hunting tribe known as the Wanderobo. This was a tribe relatively few in numbers, practising no agriculture whatever and living by hunting, by collecting honey, and by gathering wild edible fruits, seeds, and roots.

The Wanderobo peoples had already divided up this country into 'hunting territories'; each family group had its own immense zone, running sometimes to thirty or forty square miles. The boundaries were mainly geographical (prominent ridges, streams, and so on) and these were known and respected by the members of the family concerned and by the other families of Wanderobo in adjoining zones. No Wanderobo would hunt or set his traps or collect honey from any part of the country other than his own family zone and each family looked upon this zone as *personal property*.

It can be argued—in fact it has been so argued by Europeans—that the Wanderobo had not established any land property rights at all by virtue of their hunting rights, but the fact remains that they—by their own law and custom—regarded their hunting zones as their own in-violate property and, moreover, their neighbours also recognized such rights.

When the Kikuyu population increased so much in the Fort Hall district that there was need to extend farther, it was not unnatural that this virile agricultural people should look southwards to the forest and bushlands across the Chania and seek a way of obtaining land there for cul-tivation.

Undoubtedly, by virtue of their greater numerical strength, they could have driven out the Wanderobo by force, but to them such action, as we have seen, would have

3

been futile, for the land so obtained would have been valueless to them for settled occupation and for crop growing, since God and the spirits would not bless activities carried out under such conditions.

The Wanderobo for their part were envious of the easier way of life of their Kikuyu neighbours, their possession of stock and crops, which meant that the feeding of the family was much more certain than when based solely on a hunting and food-gathering way of life.

And so an entirely new system of land acquisition—new, that is to say, as far as the Kikuyu themselves and most African tribes of that day were concerned—was evolved and came into being. This is not the place to describe in great detail the very complicated processes by which a Kikuyu would enter into negotiation with a Wanderobo family for the purchase of a part of the latter's land, nor to analyse fully the way in which the purchase was transacted and the transfer of property rights completed to the satisfaction of both parties, as well as of the spirits of the departed. All these details have been dealt with by me in another book—which, however, is still unpublished—but a brief summary must be given here.

A Kikuyu elder, accompanied by a few others to act as his witnesses, could go out into the forest across the Chania and seek out a Wanderobo family, taking presents to win their friendship and carrying a bunch of grass as a sign of peaceful and honest intentions. The talk would be led round to the fact that the Kikuyu wanted land to cultivate and was willing to pay a good price in goats and sheep and other things. If, as was usually the case, the Wanderobo family was willing to part with a *portion* of its hunting zone in return for such payment, negotiations would be carried further by the Kikuyu suggesting that the two families should undertake a ceremony of 'mutual adoption' as a preliminary to the actual purchase of land and the transfer of property rights. This 'mutual adoption' was considered

4

by the Kikuyu as vital to the success of the transactions that were to be undertaken, for several reasons. In the first place, once the two families had been united by the very solemn rites of this complicated ceremony there would be no fear of treachery *by either party* during the subsequent prolonged negotiations. Secondly, the religious ceremonies which would form part of the negotiations would not be possible from the Kikuyu point of view unless all the participants were Kikuyu or adopted Kikuyu. Thirdly, the adoption ceremonies would make the departed spirits of the Wanderobo members of the Kikuyu family spirits' group and so these Wanderobo spirits would be amicably disposed towards the Kikuyu when they took over the land.

If the Wanderobo family that was first approached was unwilling to undertake 'mutual adoption' ceremonies, the Kikuyu would break off the talks and seek out some other family. But gradually the process became more and more recognized and accepted by the Wanderobo as an increasing number of Kikuyu moved south and they came to see the value of this idea to themselves.

When the ceremony of 'mutual adoption' had been successfully concluded the sale of a piece of the Wanderobo estate was carried out, the negotiations being conducted by people who now had equal status and equal obligations towards each other. At length, when the preliminaries had been completed and the due payment made, the Wanderobo family would call in members of other Wanderobo families in the region to act as witnesses to the marking of the boundaries of the piece of land that had been sold to the Kikuyu.

This marking of the boundaries was itself a very solemn religious ceremony, accompanied by sacrifices to God and to the ancestral spirits of both parties, and by prayers for blessing. Such a piece of land bought by the Kikuyu was called a *githaka* and a Kikuyu usually bought a far bigger piece of land than he required for his immediate needs, as he was setting himself up as the potential founder of a sub-clan or *mbari* all the members of which would, in due course, want a share in the ownership of that piece of land, unless they became sufficiently wealthy to go off and buy further land from other Wanderobo and start yet another *mbari* on a new *githaka*.

Coincident with the new system of acquiring land by direct outright purchase from the members of another tribe, and the consequent development of a real land-owning class, there also grew up a new system of tenant occupation or the *muhoi* system. When a wealthy Kikuyu had completed his purchase of a *githaka* from a Wanderobo, he would very soon be approached by many Kikuyu members of families still living in the Fort Hall region who were not wealthy enough to go across the Chania and buy land. They would seek permission to become tenants on the new estate with cultivation and building rights but no actual ownership. Those who made such a request would do so because of the much greater fertility of virgin forest and bush-land in the trans-Chania compared with land in Fort Hall, with the consequent chance of increased wealth and the possibility of eventually being in a position to purchase land on their own account.

From the new land-owner's point of view there were also great advantages in accepting such tenants, until such time as his own family increased so much as to need the whole estate for its own use. The presence of tenant families meant that there would be a small community living fairly close together in an *itura* or village, and so social and religious life would be able to be carried out on a normal basis. Moreover, the presence of *ahoi* (plural of *muhoi*) or tenants meant that in such work as hut-building and forest clearing the land-owner could count on man-power to help, for every such tenant had certain obligations to the land-owning family. Thus, as the purchase of estates from the Wanderobo proceeded, the land so acquired

6

became much more rapidly occupied to optimum capacity than would have happened if each estate had only been peopled by the actual land-owner and his own descendants.

This process of acquiring land across the Chania River, in what has become the Kiambu district of today, started, so far as can be estimated, in the mid-sixteenth century, and had proceeded so fast that by the closing decades of the nineteenth century the early travellers and explorers of Kenya, describing Kikuyu land as they saw it, used such terms as 'as far as the eye could see it was one vast garden'. The Kikuyu district of Kiambu also became known as the granary of the caravans that were moving up and down the country to Uganda, since it was the source of vast quantities of grain, beans, etc. There can be no doubt at all that the Kikuyu population of the Kiambu district of that time was very considerable and that cultivation was very extensive indeed.

By this time too there was only a narrow fringe of forest, varying from one to three miles wide, separating the open Athi plains, where the Masai pastoralists lived, from the Kikuyu agricultural lands that lay behind the fringe. Even the fringe itself—the forest belt—was already occupied and *owned* by Kikuyu families who had bought it from the Wanderobo. This is shown not only by the evidence of the Kikuyu themselves, but also by the references to Kikuyu fortified villages, within the forest zone, by early travellers. The evidence is reinforced by the fact that the position of a big line of fortresses in what was then the forest fringe is known, and that where these fortified villages stood, huge middens of rubbish and broken potsherds of Kikuyu type can still be identified.

This forest fringe zone of Kikuyu land, with its fortresses, had a pivot point in the region of the Muthaiga suburb of Nairobi and Ngara Road in Parklands, and ran from there along the high country bordering the plains towards the Ngong Hills via Langata Forest. On the other side it ran towards Kiambu, Ruiru, and Thika. The object of the retention of this zone by the Kikuyu as forest was quite simple. The Masai on the plains were their traditional enemies and the zone with the fortified villages formed a kind of 'Maginot Line' which made raiding expeditions by the Masai much more difficult to accomplish successfully, and therefore enhanced the security of those living in the agricultural land behind the strip.

Although this land was very fully populated, as shown by all early accounts written towards the end of the last century, it must not be imagined that it was *entirely* clear of forest and bush. It was not. Kikuyu law and custom had already laid down that considerable patches of forest must be left intact to provide timber for building and wood for fuel, and when I was a boy there were many such fuel and timber reserves set aside for the purpose, not by Government authority, but by native law.

Towards the end of the last century, then, at a time when the British were just beginning to move through the land in the days of the British East Africa Company, the Kikuyu were a big tribe living in Nyeri, Muranga (Fort Hall) and Kiambu districts, with the whole of the Kiambu district owned by individuals and families on the basis of actual purchase of huge estates or *githaka*. The occupants of the Kiambu district, however, were not all of them land-owners and the population included many who were *ahoi* or tenants.

There can be very little doubt that, had the start of white settlement in Kenya come at this particular time instead of later, very little (if any) land in Kiambu, Kabete, and Limuru would have been alienated to white farmers, for the land was carrying a big native population and no government would have tried to dispossess them for the sake of European farming.

Most unfortunately for the Kikuyu and for the future relationship between the British and the Kikuyu, the

8

position had materially changed by 1902 when the first alienation of land for farming took place on a big scale. Four major disasters had ravaged the country in the interval; the great smallpox epidemic, the great rinderpest outbreak, an intense drought with consequent famine and a devastating locust invasion. Each of these disasters is commemorated in the names given to Kikuyu initiation age-groups over this period.

As a direct consequence of these terrible events, the population was very considerably reduced. No exact figures are available, for there was no census and estimates of the death rate vary from 20 to 50 per cent. Thus the marginal Kikuyu lands, that is to say those which had been most recently acquired by purchase in the Kiambu district, (and which were also the areas most seriously affected by these catastrophes) had changed from areas with a big population to ones in which the inhabitants were very sparse. Land that had been under cultivation generally returned—as it does in Africa in a year or two—to bush, and by 1902 it could quite truthfully be said that it was hardly being used at all. This sudden and unprecedented reduction in the population and the alteration from 'one vast garden' to virtually uninhabited bushland was not only brought about by the deaths of such large numbers of the inhabitants from smallpox and famine. The reduction was accentuated by the fact that thousands of Kikuyu moved away—temporarily—from the stricken land and went back to live with relations and friends in the Nyeri and Fort Hall districts of Kikuyu country, where the drought and famine had been far less severe and the smallpox epidemic had also been less widespread.

This reduction of the population, however, did not in the least affect the *ownership* of the land. From the point of view of Kikuyu law and custom in the Kiambu district, land, even then, was not and never had been held on a communal or tribal basis but, as we have seen, was *owned*

9

by individuals and by their families through the right of inheritance. Those who moved away temporarily did not do so as an act of abandonment of their property, but because dire circumstances made such a move necessary if they were to survive at all. They looked forward to the day when they would return to develop and occupy their estate once more, and before moving away took care that even the younger men and older boys of the family knew the details of the boundaries of the family lands and could identify them. In some cases, where the family was already a large one, one unit of the family—a married son or grandson, a nephew or grand-nephew of the head of the family—was left behind while the rest moved to relatives and friends in Nyeri and Fort Hall districts, or in the remoter regions of Kiambu itself. In other cases only one or two tenant families remained behind on the large estates, pending better times and the return of the land-owning family itself.

It was at this point in Kikuyu history that the first farmer settlers, following on the heels of travellers and of missionary enterprise and the dawn of British administration, arrived upon the scene in search of land for farming and ranching and it was at this point that parts of the Kikuyu territory were alienated for white settlement, mainly during the period 1902–7.

II

MARRIAGE CUSTOMS

From this brief summary of how the Kikuyu came to move into the district now known as Kiambu and how, in the process of doing so—or more correctly as a result of doing so—they altered their law and custom in relation to land tenure and land ownership, we must turn to some other matters of practical importance in relation to the problems which form the basis upon which Mau Mau leaders have been able to build up the present position of mistrust and unrest.

We have already seen that the owners of *githaka* or estates were always willing to accept *ahoi* or tenants as occupants of part of their land with the right to cultivate and to build a home, subject to certain conditions which of course included the right to terminate the 'tenancy' with due notice. These rights which a *muhoi* obtained presented no great difficulty in the days when this system was brought into being. In the first place a Kikuyu hut was built of such materials and in such a way that its removal to a new site was an easy matter that could be accomplished in a day or so, and therefore if the owner of the land either gave the tenant notice to quit or requested him to move his homestead to some other part of the estate, no great difficulty was involved. The walls of the typical Kikuyu hut were built of heavy, hand-hewn planks of cedar and wild olive, while the rafters were made of ant-proof hardwood and the roof was thatched with bracken overlain by a thick layer of grass. No nails were used in the construction and all joints and fastenings were made with vegetable fibres. The hut so built was solid but could be taken to pieces and moved easily. For such a building it was essential that timber should be available, which was one of the reasons underlying the natives' own law, insisting on reserves of forest being retained all through the land.

Secondly, it is essential to realize that in the days when the system of *ahoi* or tenant occupiers was built up, the crops grown by the Kikuyu consisted chiefly of maize, sorghum, edible arum, bush peas, various beans, sweet potatoes, millet, bananas, and yams. With the exception of the two latter, all these were crops which lasted at the most two years before being uprooted and most of them lasted only half a year. If, therefore, a land-owner wished to give a *muhoi* notice to quit, the problem of permanent crops and compensation for them did not arise. Moreover, tree planting was not practised and if a *muhoi* encouraged the growth of natural seedlings of forest trees in the land he was cultivating, it was clearly understood that such trees were the property of the land-owner and *not* of the *muhoi* himself.

A third important thing which must be borne in mind, in relation to the conditions at the time when the British began to look for land for farming, is that in those early days the average Kikuyu family had a far greater number of goats and sheep than a similar family has today, and that the ideal grazing for goats and native sheep was *bushland and not grassland*. Cattle, of which the Kikuyu also had considerable numbers, were on the other hand, mainly grass eaters and there were extensive areas of Kikuyu country which were kept free from cultivation in order to provide grazing for cattle. To the British, whose ideas on animal husbandry were based on conditions in Great Britain, bushland looked as though it was lying idle, when in fact much of it was specifically being kept as grazing land for the goats and sheep and was just as much in beneficial use as English pasture meadows.

It will perhaps help the reader to understand the importance of goats and sheep in the social life and general economy of the Kikuyu in the days of which I am writing, if I explain that in the course of the life of an individual Kikuyu there were no less than 108 occasions from birth to death which required the slaughter and sacrifice of either a goat or a sheep, averaging about one and a half per year per member of the family. Since goats and sheep were also needed for negotiations in connexion with marriage—negotiations which have quite wrongly come to be described as 'bride purchase' and which in reality were a 'marriage insurance'—it is hardly surprising that each Kikuyu family required a fairly large herd of goats and sheep and a correspondingly big area of uncleared *bushland* (not grassland) for grazing his herds.

A brief account of Kikuyu marriage customs as they were practised in the days before the coming of the white man must next be given. It is in the breakdown of these customs that another reason can be found for the present-day discontent among the young people, a discontent which has provided fertile soil for the agitator and his anti-European propaganda.

While it would take a whole book the size of the present one to describe Kikuyu marriage customs in detail, the essentials of the underlying law and custom may be summarized as follows. When a young male Kikuyu had reached the age of marriage, he would look about among the girls who were his dancing partners at the big social dances to find one whom he felt he loved and whom he could persuade to love him. I use the word 'love' advisedly, for in choosing the woman who was to be his first and, very often, only wife, a Kikuyu was just as much concerned as any European in finding a partner with whom he thought he could be really happy.

In due course the young man would make a private proposal of marriage and if accepted he then, and only then, had to proceed according to an accepted code of rules of behaviour. This has often been mistakenly interpreted as showing that a Kikuyu bride was chosen for a young man by arrangement between the two families without the wishes of either of the young people being taken into account. This is a picture which is wholly untrue. As soon as a young man had been accepted by the girl of his choice, he would go to his father or, if his actual father was dead, to whatever man was *in loco parentis*, and would say to him in a time-honoured formula: 'My father, I want to marry a wife.' To this formula the father had to reply: 'Go away, my son, and I will consider the matter.'

The father would then proceed to make inquiries to discover where the young man's affections lay and, having found that out, he would go into the question as to whether there was any valid reason why his son should not marry the girl of his choice. Valid reasons against such a marriage would include certain ties of consanguinity, a death-bed curse made at some earlier date forbidding a marriage between the members of two families, evidence from friends that the girl in question was unstable and unlikely to make a good wife, and similar reasons. If the inquiries elicited no grounds for objecting to the marriage, the father would inform the young man's mother and if she also knew nothing adverse against the girl, the father would send for his son and speak as follows: 'My son, I have considered your request and I give you leave to choose a wife from among the following families. . . .' He would then list some half a dozen families, taking care to include the family of the girl on whom he believed his son's choice had fallen. If, however, he had discovered some reason why the proposed marriage could not be allowed, he would carefully exclude her family from the list. Should the young man find that his father had not included the family of the girl of his choice, he had the right, at this stage, to say: 'My father, will you not include the family of so and so in your list?'

It sometimes happened that the omission was due to the fact that the elder man had been misinformed as to where his son's affections lay. In such a case the request now made served to correct the error and the father's proper reply would be as follows: 'My son, go away once more and I will consider the matter and let you know if that family can be included.' If, however, the omission had been deliberate, because the marriage was held to be undesirable, he would say: 'No, my son, that family cannot be included in my list.' The young man then knew that he must abandon his idea of such a marriage as it would not receive the blessing of the family and would not be allowed to take place.

Once all this protracted method of informing the parents had been accomplished by the young man himself and had been completed satisfactorily, the subsequent proceedings had to be left to the young man's parents. It was they who inquired of the girl's family as to whether or not they, for their part, would consent to the marriage. Having obtained the necessary consent, the negotiations as to the amount of 'marriage insurance' to be paid by the bridegroom's family to the bride's family was conducted by the parents, who also fixed the day for the marriage ceremony. To the casual observer, therefore, it would seem as though the whole marriage was arranged without the young people being consulted in any way. The reasons for the handing over of the agreed number of goats and sheep (and sometimes cattle) also needs to be properly understood. Far from being a purchase, the handing over of such stock was a guarantee of good faith and of the belief on the part of the groom's family that the young man would make a good husband in accordance with law and custom. On the bride's side, the acceptance by her family of the stock was equally a guarantee that they, for their part, believed that the girl would make a good wife.

If by any chance the marriage was later to break down as a result of the failure of the young man to behave properly, then his family would be liable to forfeit all the 'marriage insurance' stock, while the wife would be permitted to go back to her own people. On the other hand, if the marriage proved a failure owing to the girl's instability and through her fault, her family would have to hand back not only the stock received as marriage insurance, but also all the computed (as distinct from its actual) offspring.

The payment and acceptance, therefore, of 'marriage insurance' was a very great factor in stabilizing marriages in a community where divorce was heavily frowned upon, and the families of both parties would take every care to try and prevent a breakdown in the marriage. If they saw signs that such an event was likely, they would go to infinite trouble to try and heal the breach before it became too serious.

Under conditions existing at the end of the nineteenth century and the early part of this century, the system worked admirably, but, as we shall see, once the European economic structure and way of life had been introduced the whole custom started to lose its original meaning. It would not be wrong to say that it has now broken down, and, far from serving its original purpose, it is having a very detrimental effect. While they are conscious that all is not well in respect of the marriages of young people today, few Kikuyu have fully realized how the breakdown has occurred, probably because they cannot look at the situation objectively. I believe, however, that the breakdown of marriage custom is a real contributory factor in the mental unrest and discontent which is, in fact, responsible for the growth of the Mau Mau movement and I shall endeavour to show how this has come about in a later chapter.

The negotiations which I have described above refer, of course, only to marriages by young men to the first or senior wife. There seems to have always been a surplus of girls, and since the social and economic structure of the tribe had no place for unmarried girls once they had passed a certain age, such surplus girls who failed to find a

16

young man who wanted them as first or senior wife had to be content with becoming second or third wives in a polygamous household. In very many cases, if a man took a second wife, he did so at the request of his senior wife, and the second wife was chosen by her from among her own personal friends who, for one reason or another, had not found a position as a senior wife. In other cases a family would find that a daughter of the house was getting on in years without contracting a marriage and would take steps to find her a husband who would accept her as second or third wife. Such marriages were by no means always unhappy, but in a sense they were *faute de mieux* and usually accepted because there was no other alternative.

A girl, however, who found herself unwooed had the right, by Kikuyu custom, to do what was called *kuheera*. She would look around for a married man with whom she felt that life as a second wife would be tolerable and then, one night, betake herself uninvited to 'his hut' and offer herself to him. If he took her in and slept with her, then it became incumbent upon him to proceed to make her legally his junior wife. The words 'his hut' need some explanation and in the explanation lies yet another reason why the changes that have taken place with the coming of modern civilization to the Kikuyu have caused so much mental unrest and instability. By Kikuyu custom, when a young man first married, he built a hut for his wife and started up a new homestead and household of his own. At the beginning, and before his wife had her first child, this might be his *only* hut, but he was expected as soon as possible, and anyhow before the birth of his first baby, to build a second hut in his new homestead—the hut which was called *thingira* or the man's hut. The first hut or *nyumba* was the sanctum of his wife—it was hers, not his— and though he could visit her in her hut and sleep with her there, he could not take his own visitors to it without her consent. If he later married a second wife, the new wife

17

had to have a separate hut of her own while the man, meanwhile, had his own hut where he entertained his male friends and where his wife or wives would bring him food for himself and his guests, but where his wife once legally married to him would not, on any account, *sleep*. A girl who decided to offer herself by the *kuheera* custom to some married man could only do so if he had a *thingira* of his own, and under no circumstances could she do so by going to him if he was sleeping in his wife's hut.

The new types of housing used by Kikuyu both in the native lands and in townships do not consist of separate huts for wife and husband and for the second wife, but rather of a different type of house altogether, divided into rooms. But this does not give the privacy that separate huts in a single homestead afforded and, in consequence, polygamy under the new conditions creates much jealousy and ill feeling, where before it seldom did. This, too, we shall discuss further in a later chapter.

Lest some readers of this book should think that the Kikuyu system gave to male partners of a marriage an unfair privilege, that of having his own hut where a girl could come and visit him and be his lover, let it be said at once that within the marriage bond a Kikuyu woman, too, had a measure of freedom and could invite a lover of her own choice (provided he was one of her husband's age-group) to *her* hut without the husband having the right to say her nay or to accuse her of unfaithfulness, provided always that she later told him openly that she had done so, just as he was expected to tell his wife of any female visitors he had entertained in his *thingira* or man's hut.

III

INITIATION CEREMONIES AND EDUCATION

We have seen how the population of Kikuyu country, and more particularly that of the Kiambu division, was very seriously reduced during the closing stages of the last century by famine and disease. The recovery from this state of affairs was at first a very slow process because Kikuyu customs at this time were of such a nature that the rate of population increase could not be very fast. We must briefly consider some of the reasons why this was the case, since the present-day picture is very different indeed and the rapid growth of population among this tribe today is another of the factors which is contributing to the conditions under which Mau Mau activities have been able to develop.

In the days before the British came to Kenya the rate of population increase was kept at a low level because, in addition to periodic epidemics such as smallpox, there were two other limiting factors operating. One of these was the very high infant mortality rate and the other the Kikuyu rule which forbade a woman to start a new child until the one she was suckling was weaned. Since children were very seldom weaned before they were two years old, babies were spaced roughly at the rate of one in three years, except where the early death of an infant had obviated the rule. One of the chief—though of course by no means the only—causes of the very high infant mortality rate, which is the second factor, was pneumonia resulting from exposure to cold night air when a child was already unwell.

By Kikuyu custom it was considered very undesirable that death should take place within a hut, although this did not matter in the case of infants who had not yet undergone the 'second birth' ceremony, during which they were supposed to be entered by the spirit of the family. Prior to this second birth ceremony a baby was regarded as merely flesh and blood which had not yet assimilated the spiritual element of the family to which he belonged. He was not yet the corporal residence of a spirit and therefore death prior to the ceremony had no bearing on the spirit world. But once a 'second birth' or 'spiritual birth' ceremony had been performed (and this was usually between the ages of one to two years, though sometimes a good deal later), if death took place inside a hut the spirit would haunt the hut until it found another home. Therefore it had to be arranged that death should take place outside. Since teething troubles and the accompanying fits, which can be linked with a not very well planned change over to solid foods, were a common occurrence at about this age, it often happened that a child who had undergone its second birth ceremony was taken ill with what appeared to the parents to be a serious illness. The child was therefore taken out of the warm hut into the cold air for fear that it should die in the hut. Not unnaturally the belief that such teething fits were very dangerous to life was strengthened by the fact that this treatment tended to make a child so exposed to a sudden change of temperature contract pneumonia and die.

The limitation of birth to one child in three years—unless the previous one had already died—was not achieved by abstinence from sexual life, but rather by the use of a method of birth control which I have discussed in detail elsewhere. Had these two factors affecting the increase of population continued in operation after the inhabitants of the Kiambu part of Kikuyu country had been so drastically reduced by famine and smallpox at the end of the last century, the population would still be small today and most of the land problems and land hunger which are causing so much concern now would not exist. But the coming of the white man and all that this meant resulted in such a major change in social custom, religious beliefs and ideas about sickness and hygiene that the rate of population increase among the Kikuyu for the past 20 or 30 years has been very high indeed.

While no one would seriously suggest that there should be any return to conditions under which the infant mortality rate was in the region (estimated) of 60 per cent of births, many medical men, social workers, and economists would like to see a return to the rule under which a woman was not allowed to ruin her own health and jeopardize the future of her own family by having children as often as nature allows. Unless birth control, wisely operated, again becomes a common Kikuyu practice, it is not easy to see what will be the economic future of this vigorous tribe of agriculturalists on the land actually and potentially available to them in the years ahead.

After a Kikuyu child had been successfully weaned and had been succeeded in the mother's care by another child, it spent a few years of comparative freedom from restraint and from duties, but when it was about eight or nine years old, whether boy or girl, the Kikuyu child started on its education. This education was both practical and theoretical. From the practical point of view, little boys at this age started to go with their elder brothers, herding the goats and sheep, trapping small game, learning the names of a host of useful plants and trees and just how to make use of their fibres, juices, gums, and so on. The little girls started to accompany their mothers on the daily round of household and agricultural duties and so also learned, in the hard school of actual practice, all the things that would make them good wives and mothers when they grew up. On the theoretical side, both boys and girls started to receive a great deal of instruction during the evenings on codes of behaviour, tribal tradition and folk lore, religion and so on. They were also taught their numerous duties with the social group to which they belonged.

This instruction, or rather education in its most real sense, was given by the elders and senior women to groups of children gathered together informally after supper. It lost nothing of its value by being informal and to a great extent voluntary, instead of being formal and compulsory. If a child did not attend the many informal talks, he or she soon found that the other children laughed at the ignorance which was bound to be noticeable as the group grew up and so, since the laughter of one's playmates is one of the hardest things to bear, few if any children grew up without this fundamental education to fit them for their place in tribal life.

As the period of puberty approached, the tempo of the education of both boys and girls was greatly increased. In addition to attending the talks by senior members of the village in the evenings, they were expected to learn the steps and tunes of the various traditional dances and songs, to show in their behaviour that they had learnt and absorbed the rules of manners that they had been taught verbally in earlier childhood and, above all, to learn to behave in such a way that they could claim to qualify for the initiation rites which would turn them, in the eyes of the tribe, from children into young adults—full members of the tribe and of the clan with full responsibilities as well as benefits. In Kikuyu society no one could claim the benefits of adult status and full membership of the tribe and age-group unless he or she was also willing to accept a share in the responsibilities which such status brought with it. Once initiation and the subsequent period of the novitiate had been passed, boys and girls, now young men and women, would be bound by the will of the majority of their age-group and could only go against such will at the risk of complete ostracism.

22

When the time came for the actual initiation ceremonies, of which the circumcision operation on the males and the comparable female operation was only the 'outward and visible sign', the whole ceremony was planned to extend the education of the young people to fit them for citizenship and the responsibilities of adult life. The details of all these ceremonies will be found in another and fuller book of mine. Let it suffice to say here that the initiation rites were of a prolonged character and linked with the religious beliefs and practices of the tribe. They also included ceremonies of a symbolic nature, to fix in the minds of the initiates the nature of their various duties to the tribe and to their elders, which they were about to assume. Most unfortunately, in the fifty-two years of the present century, economic and many other factors have reduced the initiation rites of the Kikuyu to nothing more than the hurried performance of the 'outward and visible sign' of the achievement of adult status—the operations of circumcision and cliterodectomy. All the character-training and preparation for the responsibilities of tribal membership have ceased to be inculcated during the initiation and pre-initiation period. This development was inevitable, but it is a pity that some other really adequate substitute in character-training and citizenship has not been organized to replace what has been lost.

The old training would anyhow not serve to prepare youth for the responsibilities of life as it is today, but it would certainly have been better than nothing. If no substitute could be devised, it would at least have continued to teach respect for constituted authority and the need to serve the community even at the expense of individual wishes. It would also have taught the advantages of good manners, honesty and sobriety. It can thus be said that the failure to find an adequate substitute for the character-training and preparation for citizenship, which the age-old Kikuyu initiation rites used to give, is just one

23

more underlying cause of the present sad state of affairs in the Kikuyu tribe.

From the completion of the initiation ceremony proper, until the whole new age-group had been brought into being, the boys and girls were ranked as 'novices' and were considered to be in an 'unclean state' and also to be without sex. During this period the young initiates wandered about in bands, practising the dances of the tribe, visiting friends and relatives, soliciting gifts and testing each other—quiz fashion—on the laws and customs which they had been taught.

At length the day came when the novitiate was ended by ceremonial purification carried out by the elders and medicine men of the districts in which the novices lived; they then became full members of an age-group of their own and as such began to live a corporate life which transcended family and clan obligations and was linked with tribal responsibilities. The young men now had to devote a part of their lives to military training under senior warriors and, when called to do so, they took part in raids upon the Masai or in defensive battles with their traditional enemies. The age-group, too, began to seek among its own members enough outstanding personalities to appoint a governing council of the group, from which delegates would attend the councils of the senior warrior group and so learn how to conduct tribal business in relation to the affairs of youth.

The girls, now recognized as full adults, were liable to various types of communal labour in conjunction with the older women, while they also began to look about for husbands, not among the youths of their own age-group and with whom they had undergone the initiation ceremonies, but rather among the men of the senior warrior group who would soon be destined to pass on to the status of junior or 'first-grade elder'.

Dancing, especially at times of full moon, now occupied a

great deal of the time of these girls and they also learned from the older girls of the senior age-group how to dress their hair in proper and attractive style, how to decorate themselves with red ochre and how to behave towards young men with decorum and yet to be attractive. It was a common feature of the relationship of young men and girls to sleep in the same bed together at this stage of their career, but full sexual intercourse was prohibited, and, if indulged in before marriage and found out, was heavily punished. Moreover, the age-group itself felt so strongly that the breaking of this law would bring disgrace not only on the guilty individual but on the whole age-group, that the members took good care to mete out such drastic punishment to any member who looked as though he or she might break this law, that temptation to do so was reduced to a minimum. Today, in contrast, young men and girls who have achieved adult status within the tribe by the 'outward and visible sign' of the operation which marks the change of status, but who have absorbed none of the character-training and laws of society which should accompany such a step, indulge in similar familiarities but, in the absence of the corporate spirit of the old age-group system and the controls that the family imposed, frequently allow such amusements to lead to full sexual intercourse. The number of unmarried mothers among the Kikuyu is increasing alarmingly and is also playing its part in the rising tempo of insecurity and discontent within the tribe.

It is a truism that for man and woman in civilized society education ends only with the grave, but at least for the majority of us, our education after we have passed the examination stage in our early twenties or earlier, is a voluntary matter. But for the Kikuyu—as indeed for almost all Bantu-speaking peoples in the days before we brought western ideas to the country—the whole of life was marked by a series of *rites de passage*, as the social anthropologist calls them, in other words stages, through which the

25

individual must pass. Each of these was marked to a greater or lesser degree by tests of his ability to sustain the status of the next upward stage in the hierarchy.

In due course the junior warrior became a senior warrior and then in a short time he qualified for marriage and, having married, he passed out into the status of first grade or 'junior elder', usually as soon as he had become not merely a husband but also a father. While the ceremony marking this stage of transition was less complex than that which he had undergone when he first entered adult status and was usually only enacted on a local village basis, nevertheless the undergoing of the ceremony marked the entry into a new stage of his actual education. As a first-grade elder, the young man must now start to learn the copious tribal case-law of his region, must learn to speak well in public debates and, above all, must learn the art of cross-examining witnesses, so that in due course as a second-grade elder he could take his turn on the various local and district *kiamas* or councils and help to administer justice, and perhaps eventually qualify as a judicial expert. Naturally not all achieved the same proficiency in these arts, and it was to those who succeeded best that the highest honours would eventually be awarded.

Every first-grade elder, too, had to start learning a great deal more about the conduct of sacrifice to God, to the ancestral spirits and to the spirits of trees and waterfalls, first as a spectator at such ceremonies, then as an actual associate, so that when the time came he would be able to officiate himself in family and regional acts of worship should he be called upon to do so.

The girls, for their part, had a *rite de passage* when they passed from the status of girl to married woman, and yet another at the birth of the first child. For both men and women the last stage of their education only came when they had eventually become grandparents and thus earned the right to some of the highest religious and secular offices

26

in the community, as well as to certain privileges which no others could attain.

For the Kikuyu this long process of education was wholly lacking in some of the things that we, mistakenly perhaps, include under that all-embracing head. For example there was no training in reading, writing, and arithmetic. Education consisted of an organized series of stages of preparation for the responsibilities of life in the community to which the individual belonged. As such, it was fundamental education which made good citizens, honest men and women, and wise parents and leaders of the community, in which a sense of responsibility to those in the lower grades and to the tribe as a whole was very strongly developed.

IV

SOCIAL ORGANIZATION

The fabric of Kikuyu social organization was a complex one
in which two distinct patterns can be clearly traced. On
the one hand there was an organization founded upon a
patriarchal system in which the basic unit was the extended
family. This system was closely linked with land ownership.
We have already seen that as the Kikuyu moved into trans-
Chania—a process which started probably in the sixteenth
century—individuals bought land with a view to becoming
the founders of sub-clans or *mbari* as they are called. By the
end of the nineteenth century these *mbari*, tracing their
origin to a single individual land-owner, were each represented by a large number of people. Such a land-owning
sub-clan, which might consist of a thousand adults or more,
was regarded as a social unit which was bound together
not only by ties of consanguinity, but by complex rules and
regulations. The head of a group, during the lifetime of the
original founder, was of course the founder himself, but
thereafter he was appointed by the adult male members
of the sub-clan, not by an election on a voting system such
as would be used in western countries, but on a basis of discussion until unanimity was reached.

The head so appointed was not by any means necessarily
the senior living male member of the group, but he was
chosen rather for his wisdom, tact, and also suitability as a
religious leader; the head of the sub-clan, who was known as
the *muramati*, had many religious as well as secular duties to
perform for the group. Whenever any matter affecting the
sub-clan as a whole cropped up, it was the duty of this
titular head to call together the adult male members of the
group to discuss the matter and reach a solution. If any

individual member of the sub-clan, all of whom were land-owners having a share in the one single estate or *githaka*, wished to introduce a tenant on to that portion of the land which he occupied and controlled, he had first of all to get the sanction of the titular head as the living representative of the original sole owner of the estate, i.e. the founder of the sub-clan.

In a sense the titular head, who was chosen unanimously by the members of the sub-clan, ranked as the *owner* of the estate and was often spoken of as such, while at the same time it was recognized that all the male descendants were part-owners and had absolute right to their own share of it. Such individuals could, if they so wished, and if their circumstances necessitated it, dispose outright of their portion of the family estate by sale, although such action was always discouraged. But if an individual did wish to take such a drastic step, it was laid down that he *must* first tell the titular head of his intention. This man would then be responsible for trying to find one of the members of the sub-clan who would be willing to buy, so that the estate, as a whole, remained an entity belonging to the sub-clan and thus no part of it would go outside the family. Only if no other member of the sub-clan could be found who was willing to purchase could an individual be given permission by the titular head to sell to an outsider.

This particular rule is of considerable importance to our understanding of some of the problems of the present-day unrest. In some cases it has been claimed that land was purchased outright by Europeans, in the days of the 1902–7 alienation, from individual members of a land-owning sub-clan who had remained in residence on a *githaka* when the others had temporarily moved away, for the reasons that have been outlined in chapter two. From the point of view of the Kikuyu, such sales, if they took place, were invalid and contrary to native law and custom unless they had been approved by the titular head of the

29

estate concerned and after other members of the sub-clan had been given a first option to purchase. Moreover, no individual member of such a sub-clan—unless he was the last surviving male descendant of the original founder—could sell more than his own small share of the family estate.

In all matters of dispute between members of the same sub-clan, it was the council of elders drawn from members of that sub-clan who would hear the case and make a decision. No elders of other sub-clans could take a part in such proceedings unless they had been specifically invited to do so—by consent of both parties of the dispute—because of their special wisdom or because of particular knowledge of the matter under dispute.

When any religious ceremony or sacrifice either to God or to the ancestral spirits of the sub-clan had to be performed, it was the titular head who officiated and those male members of the sub-clan who had attained the necessary grade in the elders' hierarchy who took part or formed the audience. In other words, in all matters concerning land, religion, law, etc., which were the concern only of the sub-clan members and affecting no outsider or third party, the sub-clan organization stood apart and alone.[1] Within the larger sub-clans—and many of them were very large—there were often sub-sub-clans which had their own similar organization to that of the sub-clan as a whole. In matters only affecting members of such a sub-sub-clan and in which no members of other sub-sub-clans were involved, the members of such a smaller group within the larger one could act alone *except in matters relating to land*.

Lower down the scale was each individual and 'extended' family, of which the head was the 'father', using the term

[1] Since nearly every *githaka* or estate held by a *mbari* or sub-clan had *ahoi* or tenants who did not belong to the group living on the same estate, the second pattern of social organization, which will be described later and which was on a territorial and not a consanguinity basis, came into being.

in the African classificatory sense (which will be outlined presently) and not in the strict sense of relationship. Thus a sub-clan or a sub-sub-clan was composed of a number of 'extended family units', consisting of the head of the family or father and his children and possibly grandchildren and even great-grandchildren in the case of very old men, using all these terms in the African and not the strict European sense. Within such a family the organization was the same as that of a sub-clan, in that the head of the family—even when his sons and grandsons were grown up and had homesteads of their own—was the person who had to be consulted in all matters and who had to convene meetings of family members to discuss affairs affecting the family. He was also responsible for conducting religious worship and performing sacrifices for all the members of the family so long as he was alive. The only main difference between the family organization of such matters and that of the sub-clans and sub-sub-clans was that the head of the family owed his position to seniority, while the head of the other bigger groups was chosen for his suitability for the position.

I have stated that the head of a family was the 'father' in the extended African classificatory sense and not in our European sense. African ideas of family relationship must now be outlined briefly. This is not easy to do and few Europeans ever fully comprehend the intricacies of the Kikuyu system. If what follows (and which is only a summary of a system which would take a hundred pages to describe) sounds to the reader fantastic, it will at least, I hope, make him realize how different African ideas are from ours and how easy it is therefore for serious misunderstandings to arise between black and white.

The term 'brother' is extended to all of a man's brothers and half-brothers and also to his male first cousins on his father's side. All of these men ranked as 'father' to the males of the next generation. Thus, if the actual father of a

family died, his next senior brother, half-brother or patrilineal first cousin became *automatically* 'father' to those whose
real father had died. It was not until there was no male
member of that generation left alive that the responsibilities
would devolve on to the respective eldest sons of each of
the men in the earlier group. From having been one family,
the extended family would then break up into as many new
families as there had originally been male members of the
earlier generation. This sounds somewhat complicated, but
in practice it worked very easily and smoothly.

The fundamental basis of the Kikuyu classificatory system
is to be found in three equations which are: (1) I and my
grandfather are one; (2) I and my brother and my sister are
one; (3) I and my wife are one. Anyone who takes the
trouble to sit down with paper, a good many hours of spare
time, and a good head for mathematics, and draws out a
large hypothetical family tree covering five generations, can
then with the help of these equations at once sort out the
relationship in the Kikuyu system of any person in the tree
to the other.

Let me give just one example which will, I hope, help to
explain how the 'father' of an extended family is plural.
Since 'I and my grandfather are one', and since 'I and my
brother are one', it follows that not only am I one with my
brother, but also with all my half-brothers and all my male
cousins on the paternal side. For clearly, if I and my
brother are one, this also applies to my grandfather and his
brothers, therefore I am one with my grandfather's brothers.
But my grandfather's brothers are one with their grandsons, and therefore I am one with these grandsons who are
my first cousins in the patrilineal line.

It thus follows that all the brothers, half-brothers and
male cousins on the patrilineal side are one person, and it is
this 'one person', who is yet many people, who is the head
or 'father' of the family, the headship resting for convenience
in the senior living member of such a generation group

until all the members of that generation group are dead. It is this complicated classificatory system (which is so little understood by most Europeans in Kenya) that lies at the root of many problems and misunderstandings in the relations between black and white today, and strangely enough which has also been responsible for the erroneous belief that most Kikuyu men in the olden days were highly polygamous.

It is, of course, true that owing to the surplus of women over men, and owing to the aversion of women to remaining unmarried beyond a certain age, polygamy did exist and we have already in an earlier chapter seen how second and third wives were chosen, or in some cases chose their own husbands. But the picture which was sometimes given by early travellers of men with a vast number of wives, and of nearly every married man having several wives, was in large part due to a misunderstanding of the Kikuyu family classificatory system.

By this system, and because of the equations which have been given above, a man referred to and addressed all those women who were the wives of his classificatory self, i.e. of his brothers, half-brothers and patrilineal cousins, as 'my wife'. This term was also extended to the wives of his grandfather and his classificatory grandfathers, or to the wives of his grandsons if they were old enough to be married. Thus, if a visitor to a Kikuyu village pointed to some women standing around and asked who they were, all those who stood in this relationship to the man of whom the question was asked would be described to him as 'my wife'; some of these might be very old women, wives of the man's grandfather, others quite young. Moreover, the Kikuyu firmly believed that Europeans had the same classificatory system (since it would never occur to him that any other classificatory system of family relationships could exist) and would therefore not think it necessary to explain that they were not his actual physical wives. The truth was, further, that by

33

native law a man could not so much as touch with one finger—let alone be intimate with—any of the many women whom he referred to and addressed as 'my wife' (except, of course, his own legal and physical wife) without incurring penalties.

I commenced this chapter by saying that I would describe the two distinct patterns in the fabric of Kikuyu social organization, but it has been necessary to digress in order to describe the way in which social, religious, land, and other matters were dealt with in all cases where the persons concerned were all members of one sub-clan or sub-sub-clan, or of one of the 'extended families' of which the other two groups were composed. I must now pass on to the other pattern of social structure.

We have already seen that the land of the Kikuyu was divided into three main divisions: Muranga (or Fort Hall as it is now called), Nyeri and Kiambu. These ranked as *bururi* and they were territorial units with convenient geographical boundaries forming the major divisions of Kikuyu country. Each of these three major units was further divided into a large number of smaller territorial units called *rugongo*. These consisted of all the land lying between two lesser geographical boundaries such as streams. The word *rugongo* means, strictly, a ridge and in many cases it was simply the ridge of land lying between and separating two streams and probably extending for 20 or 30 miles. For political purposes, however, a *rugongo* sometimes covered more than one ridge in the strictly geographical sense. In this chapter we shall use the term *rugongo* in its political and administrative sense.

These territorial units or 'ridges' bore no relation whatever to the land-owner units or estates, for it often happened that one single estate was so situated that it lay across several different ridges. Equally either the whole or parts of many different estates might be included in one single ridge unit. For all tribal, as distinct from sub-clan, affairs,

34

for purposes of law, religious worship, warfare and all else affecting members of the tribe irrespective of their sub-clan status, the ridge was the most important administrative unit of this second pattern in social organization, which had been set up to co-ordinate the affairs of each ridge within one of the three major territorial divisions of Kikuyu territory.

Had the system of 'chiefs' in the sense in which Europeans use that term and know it in other parts of Africa existed among the Kikuyu in the days before the coming of the white man, each of these ridges would probably have ranked as the area of a single chief. But the Kikuyu had no 'chief' system and each ridge was administered and controlled by a council of senior elders, the leading member of which council was known by the title of *muthamaki*, a term frequently misinterpreted as 'chief', which really meant 'spokesman for the senior council'. Such a spokesman was not a chief in our English sense at all; he was simply the 'chairman of the council of nine' in whom authority rested (both secular and religious), and it was he who would be the chosen *spokesman* for the ridge in any talks or negotiations with foreign visitors. But he was *not* a 'chief', he had no personal authority and was only the spokesman of the senior council, which in turn only owed its authority to the powers vested in it by subsidiary councils further down the scale.

The senior council of nine or the *kiama kinene* of each ridge was appointed by the subsidiary councils of nine which controlled the affairs of the various *mwaki* or subsidiary divisions of a ridge. The term *mwaki* means literally 'fire' and the territorial and administrative unit known as a *mwaki* owed its name to the fact that it represented a group of villages the inhabitants of which had 'fire' in common. That is to say that, within such a unit, any person whose fire had gone out in his hut could get a new fire going by fetching hot embers from any other hut within the same unit without

35

contravening law and custom. If he could not do so, for some reason, he must kindle a fresh fire by means of fire sticks and under no circumstances must he fetch fire from the hut of any other *mwaki* or administrative unit. We shall therefore refer to the administrative unit which a Kikuyu calls a *mwaki* by the term 'fire-linked unit'.

The councils of each 'fire-linked unit' were appointed by the lesser councils of nine which controlled the affairs of each *itura* or village group within a given fire-linked unit. In any affair or dispute or religious ceremony that affected only the members of a given village, the council of that village acted. In affairs which affected persons of more than one village, but all of the same fire-linked unit, it was that council that was responsible. If there was any matter which affected persons of more than one fire-linked unit within the ridge, but all of the same ridge, then the ridge council took the matter in hand.

There were, of course, occasions when there were disputes, or when religious matters arose which affected persons other than those belonging to a particular ridge, and then a *special ad hoc* council of nine would be convened for the occasion. On it would sit representatives of each and all the ridges involved. This simple and yet highly effective organized system of decentralized control of religious, judicial, and secular affairs was not in the least understood by the British when they came to the country. The administrators believed that throughout Africa there was a system of 'chiefs' and sub-chiefs and they believed wrongly that the spokesman of the senior ridge councils was the 'chief' of that ridge. If he met with approval he was retained as 'chief' whereas he had never before been a chief in our sense, and if he did not suit the British he was replaced by a 'chief' chosen and appointed by the administration. Thus there was instituted a system wholly foreign to Kikuyu custom and tradition, but it was one which the particular person chosen to hold the rank of 'chief' under the British

Government liked very much, for it gave him individual powers which he had never held before.

Although in theory the councils of the respective ridges, fire-linked units, and villages were also responsible for the actual administration of justice, it was recognized by the Kikuyu that the hearing of complicated law suits was one which needed special knowledge of the law and special wisdom. In practice, therefore, when acting in its judicial capacity a council of nine always called in elders who had specially qualified as 'judges', to take part with them in their work and guide them by their knowledge of 'case law' which was, of course, oral and traditional and not written law. In the earlier days of the administration there was no interference with the practice, save that often a 'chief', by virtue of the office he held by government authority and not tribal custom, would insist on participating in the proceedings of a council sitting in its judicial capacity, although by law and custom he was not qualified to do so.

Subsequently, Government introduced a system of 'tribunals' and although sometimes (owing to wise advice) the members of such 'tribunals' were chosen from men qualified in native eyes to hold such a judicial post, this was by no means always the case. And so gradually an entirely new system of administration has been foisted upon the Kikuyu and is now an accepted part of their present-day organization, although there are many among the senior elders who still doubt whether the new system works better than, or even as well as, the old.

Certainly there is far less respect for government 'chiefs' and government appointed headmen than there used to be for the opinions of councils constituted under the law and custom of the tribe. In fairness, however, it must be said that this is not wholly because the new system is less good than the old, or less honoured than the old. It is in part due to the fact that there has been a complete breakdown in the whole social system and a change over to rank individualism, instead of each person being merely a part of a well-knit unit, each member of which had well-defined responsibilities one to the other. The breakdown of the old system of authority and the failure up till now of the new system to get fully into its stride and to have become really accepted by the masses, has certainly been a contributory factor in making the present outbreak of lawlessness— fermented by the Mau Mau—possible.

V

RELIGIOUS BELIEFS

In the preceding chapter we have referred to the fact that the conduct of religious worship and the performance of sacrifices, both to God and to the ancestral spirits, were the function of various people such as the *muramati* or titular head of a sub-clan, the senior council of nine of a *rugongo* or ridge and of the 'father' or head of an 'extended family', according to the nature of the particular act of worship or sacrifice that was to be performed.

It is now necessary to consider a little more fully the basic Kikuyu religious ideas and practices, as they were at the time of the coming of European civilization, for here again the breakdown of the old system and the substitution of other religious ideas has also played its part, and in some cases a very large part, in the present Mau Mau situation.

Just as the fabric of Kikuyu social organization had a dual overlapping and in some cases interlocking pattern, so, too, we find that Kikuyu religious beliefs seem to represent the interweaving of three distinct religious concepts which sometimes overlap and sometimes are interlocked. First, there is the belief in *Murungu* or, as he is also called, *Ngai*, who is God, supreme, almighty, unseen but all pervading, having four 'homes' in the four sacred mountains of the Kikuyu (Kenya, the Aberdare Range, the Ngong Hills, and Juja Hill). While residing at one and the same time in these four mountains, he is yet present everywhere. This God of the Kikuyu was anthropomorphic and had many human attributes; whereas he liked to be worshipped from time to time in acts of communal worship and sacrifice, he could nevertheless be spoken to and prayed to, by any individual.

While long prayers to God by the individual were rare, no good Kikuyu adult in the days before the coming of the white man would go to sleep in his hut without saying the words '*Ngai ndaria*', which means 'God keep me through this night', nor would he omit in the morning, when he woke, to say, '*Ngai niwandaria*', 'God you have kept me through this night', thereby acknowledging his safe keeping to God.

Whenever there was an act of family worship, whether linked with birth, or harvest, or marriage, or sickness in the cattle, or any other matter, the prayers and sacrifices that would be made to the ancestral spirits of the family were always preceded by a brief prayer to God. This God, *Ngai* or *Murungu*, was to some extent linked in the minds of the Kikuyu with the sun, and prayers to God were often said as the sun rose above the skyline at dawn, but the worship of *Ngai* was not a real 'sun worship' as it is in some other parts of Africa. Certain things do suggest, however, that the concept of God, as it was fifty years ago in this tribe, had been modified from an earlier more thorough-going sun worship. In every *rugongo* territorial unit of the ridge category there was one fig tree set aside which was the special place of communal worship of God and the place for the performance of sacrifice to him. Around and about such a fig tree, bushes and shrubs were allowed to grow and there were often also subsidiary fig trees so that the place was virtually a 'sacred grove'.

No branch of any sacred fig tree of such a place of worship could be cut, nor any of the surrounding shrubs and bush growth cut down, nor could goats and sheep be allowed to go near, nor women and children approach at all close. Any person who desecrated such a place was subject to dire punishment, and the sacred grove also had much of the old Hebrew idea of a 'place of sanctuary'. A fugitive from justice or from an angry enemy could not be dragged out if he sought refuge in such a grove, nor could he be attacked and killed within the sacred grove.

When sacrifices were made to God, whether in a village, fire-linked unit, or ridge basis, the officiating elders would call together the people concerned to the place of worship and there perform their sacrifice of a ram of one colour and without blemish. Part of the blood and part of the meat was offered to God and left at the foot of the tree for him, while the rest was consumed on the spot by the participants, the bones being burnt at the foot of the tree as an offering when the sacrificial feast was completed.

Worship of God not only consisted of act of supplication and prayer for relief of drought or epidemic, etc., but also in acts of thanksgiving for good harvests, for rain sent in answer to prayer and so on. In fact, in very many ways, the Kikuyu worship of God differed not very greatly from that of the Hebrews in Old Testament times.

The second pattern of Kikuyu religious belief was that which was wholly concerned with the worship and placating of the departed ancestral spirits. It must here be explained that the Kikuyu believed that a person had two kinds of spirit, one of which on his death passed into the company of the family ancestral spirits, while the other was a sort of communal family spirit which was both single and yet multiple. This family spirit was present as a separate entity in every member of the family who had undergone the 'second birth' or 'spiritual birth' ceremony in his or her childhood, and yet a part of the same family spirit was always in the air, hovering near and waiting for the birth of a new member of the family to take up corporal residence through the sacred rite of the 'second birth' ceremony until death should intervene.

The worship of ancestral spirits was principally linked with family, sub-clan and sub-sub-clan religious ceremonies. It also had a part in ceremonies that were not connected with such consanguinal groups, since each participant in a ceremony of sacrifice to God was always conscious of the ever-present spirits of his own departed ancestors and

41

relatives. Prayers and acts of worship to God were always followed, therefore, by prayers to the spirits of the various participant families. Moreover, and this is important, the ancestral spirits were always linked with the living in the prayers of the supreme deity.

The special places of residence of the ancestral spirits were in the hearth-stones of the huts in which the people lived and also in the courtyards of the homesteads, at the special tree in the courtyard where it was customary to hang up bunches of sweet-potato vine for the sheep and goats to eat in the evening, when they came back from the pastures.

In other words ancestral spirits, like God, had special places of residence as well as being all-pervading and everywhere. Whenever food was eaten, small bits were first broken and dropped on the ground, preferably near the hearth-stones, and at the same time a brief prayer was uttered. Whenever beer was drunk, or milk or blood, a little was poured out on the ground as a libation to the ancestral spirits. Whenever a ram, a virgin ewe, or a goat was slaughtered in connexion with some ceremonial act at birth or at any of the other very numerous occasions when such a sacrifice was necessary, a part of the sacrificial animal was set aside for the spirits.

At every marriage ceremony the spirits of the families of bride and bridegroom were joined to the living members of the family in the religious act that set the seal on the marriage, so that the respective families were united in blessing the marriage by the consent of all the members of the family, both living and in the spirit world. Religion in the form of ancestor worship in fact pervaded every act of family life. Every individual member of the family from the earliest days of his or her instruction from the elders to the days when life was ending, felt himself or herself closely united to and linked with the unseen spirit members of the family group.

Many forms of sickness and ill-health, many of the minor disasters of daily life, were explained not by natural causes, nor yet as acts of vengeance by God, but by the disapproval of the ancestral spirits for some act of commission or omission which had displeased them. It was therefore incumbent upon all members of the family to abide closely by the rules of behaviour and code of morals of the tribe in order to avoid the displeasure of the departed.

The third pattern that can be discerned in the fabric of Kikuyu religious practice is that which is connected with the belief in certain spirits that are not in any way 'human', nor yet linked with the concept of God—the spirits of such things as trees, large isolated rocks, waterfalls, and also epidemic diseases. Possibly this animistic religion was the oldest of the three superimposed and often interlocked patterns of religious belief. It certainly played a rather less important part in the life of the community than did either the worship of God or of the ancestral spirits; it was less a matter of worship than of placating an unseen and little understood supernatural force that was not connected with God or the ancestral spirits. This animistic aspect of religion was reflected in a very large number of ceremonies and one example will serve to illustrate this.

When a Kikuyu started clearing a fresh patch of forest, or woodland, he always left certain large trees unfelled to provide a home for the spirits of all the trees that he was cutting down. The cutting down of the trees would be started some distance away from the tree selected to remain standing as the home of tree-spirits, so that as the felling approached closer and closer the tree-spirits would move in towards the selected tree. As each tree was cut, a prayer would be uttered to its spirit asking it to move farther and find a new home. Eventually the spirits of all the felled trees were believed to be concentrated in the few large trees

43

left standing. A small lamb would be sacrificed to the tree-spirits and offered to them at the foot of these trees with a request for blessing.

If ever at some future date it became necessary to fell one of these isolated trees that had been made into a tree-spirit home, a most elaborate ceremony had to be performed before the tree could be cut down. A group of elders would approach the tree, usually at sundown, and perform a sacrifice. They would then place a branch from some other tree against the bole of the tree that was to be cut down and pray to the tree's spirit to forgive them for what they would have to do. They would also ask the tree-spirits to enter the branch over night so that they might be conveyed next morning to some new home. At dawn a procession would solemnly carry this branch and lay it against the bole of some other large tree in the district.

From all that has been said in this chapter, and it is only the barest outline of Kikuyu religious ideas and practices, it will be readily understood that the Kikuyu were a deeply religious people for whom life without religion was unthinkable. It was to such a people that the missionaries, Protestants and Catholic alike, came towards the closing stages of the nineteenth century, bringing with them the many variations of the Christian doctrine and dogma. How these new ideas affected the Kikuyu, how they were received, and how they led in many cases to the setting up of strongly separatist churches, partly Christian and partly pagan, will be discussed later, for this, too, has a most important bearing upon the problem of the growth of the Mau Mau movement and its anti-Christian bias.

Closely linked with the religious beliefs of the Kikuyu was the concept of guilt and spiritual uncleanness, brought about by breaking of law and custom, of taboos and of religious injunctions, whether deliberately or quite involuntarily, and from which a person could only be freed by an act of 'ceremonial purification'. Such spiritual uncleanness was, in fact, seldom risked voluntarily, for while such a state existed, and before cleansing, it was a serious menace to the health and well-being of the person concerned.

Often a man or woman would be wholly unaware of having done something which rendered them spiritually unclean, and their first indication of it would be in a feeling of malaise, perhaps of persistent headaches, or pains in the joints which we in our modern knowledge would ascribe to some physical ailment. For the Kikuyu such symptoms, if persistent, suggested some supernatural cause and a 'medicine man' would be consulted. Sometimes the trouble was diagnosed as having been caused by the displeasure of ancestral spirits and a sacrifice of appeasement would be performed. More often the trouble would be traced to some unwitting breaking of a taboo that had brought about a state of spiritual uncleanness, and then an act of ceremonial purification had to be performed.

There were very many variations of ceremonial purification which cannot be described in detail here; all of them involved the slaughter of a ram, a ewe, or a lamb and the drinking of a concoction which contained part of the undigested stomach contents of the sacrificed animal, the placing of a wristlet of raw hide from the same animal on the arm, and the smearing of the patient with the stomach contents. The other complicated details of the varying rituals that accompanied the purification differed according to what had caused the initial uncleanness.

Under certain circumstances the taking of some types of oath could cause a state of spiritual uncleanness and when this was so, a person could be 'cleansed' from the effects of the oath by an act of ceremonial purification. This, too, is a matter of great importance in connexion with the Mau Mau disturbances, for the oath taken is of such a nature that it is possible to be freed from its effects by voluntary

45

submission to a cleansing ceremony, properly performed. More particularly is this true where the oath in question was taken in some manner contrary to established law and custom and native practices, which in fact is the case with every, or nearly every, Mau Mau oath.

VI

MAGIC: WHITE AND BLACK

It is not easy to draw a dividing line between religion and magic in Kikuyu society, nor between white magic which is beneficial and black magic or witchcraft which is anti-social. The Kikuyu methods of administering oaths are intimately connected with the belief in magic and witchcraft and some understanding of the effect of oaths is essential if we are to fathom the methods which have been so successfully used by Mau Mau.

The Kikuyu worker in white magic, whom many people would call a 'medicine man', was known as a *mundu mugo*. His rôle in tribal organization was a composite one; he was the doctor who diagnosed and treated diseases and ailments, sometimes by herbal remedies, sometimes by magic rites and purification ceremonies and sometimes by a combination of both. He was also the seer who was consulted as to whether the occasion was propitious for marriage, for a long journey, or for the holding of an initiation ceremony, and he was the person whose help was sought against the workers in black magic or witchcraft who tried to destroy people and property and who were known as *murogi*.

The workers in white magic, or medicine men, held a very honoured place in the tribe and membership of the guild was confined to persons who had served a long apprenticeship before being finally accepted to this calling. Moreover, a man who wished to stand for the profession had to satisfy the other members of the guild that he had a special 'calling' for such work before he could even become an apprentice or trainee. These medicine men were always of outstanding ability and great wisdom, and although their profession gave them no special rights to other functions in the tribal organization, it was not uncommon to find that a medicine man was also one of the people chosen to officiate in the more important religious ceremonies, not necessarily because he was a medicine man, but because of his general outstanding qualities.

As a medical practitioner, the medicine man often became somewhat of a specialist and so it was common to find that one was renowned for his knowledge of herbs and his treatment of special types of illness, while another might be sought out more often to diagnose obscure maladies and treat them by the method of discovering what form of 'spiritual uncleanness' the patient was suffering from and then conduct a suitable purification ceremony to remove the cause of ill. The herbal specialists certainly had a very considerable knowledge of the healing properties of various plants and their juices and fruits, some of which would undoubtedly repay a careful study by our own medical research workers. The man who specialized in tracing the causes of malaise to supernatural events and then bringing about a cure by cleansing was really a very clever practitioner in psychotherapy.

Every medicine man during his period of training learnt the art of using the divining gourd and every one of them had his own divining gear or *mwano*. Any medicine man, therefore, whether he was a specialist in herbal remedies or in the curing of ills by ceremonial purification, was also a seer who could be consulted on almost any matter. But here again there were specialists who had earned a high reputation for accurate prophecy and it was to such men that the elders or the army leaders went when they wanted advice as to whether a particular date was propitious for the start of an important initiation ceremony or for the sending out of a raiding party against the Masai.

There were also medicine men who were specialists in protective magic—magic to prevent black-magic workers from exercising their powers to harm the members of a

48

homestead; to protect cattle, goats, and sheep from disease; to protect crops from thieves and to make charms to give the wearer security against evil eye, against dangers from wild beasts, and from death in battle.

The services of a medicine man, in no matter what capacity, were always subject to the payment of a fee of one kind or another and a consultation also usually involved the slaughter of a ram or a virgin ewe, to be provided by the person seeking help and advice. This served to prevent anybody from seeking the aid of a medicine man unless he felt his need was very great. Belief in the powers of the medicine man was absolute, and if a cure failed or a pro-phecy was not fulfilled, it was not the medicine man who was blamed for incompetence. It was believed rather that some still stronger agency was at work to counteract the magic powers invoked, and so further magic aid would be called in.

It should perhaps be noted here that even when herbal remedies with true therapeutic properties were used, it was the 'magic' of these remedies that was believed to be potent. For the vast majority of the Kikuyu, therefore, the drugs which have been introduced by modern medicine are also considered as 'magic' remedies and the medical officer simply as a *mundu mugo*. Even the apparatus of modern medical science used in diagnosis—such as the stethoscope and thermometer—rank for the masses as simply the white man's methods of diagnosis comparable to the medicine man's use of his divining gourd to discover whether an ailment has been brought about by spiritual uncleanness, and, if so, of what kind.

Whereas a *mundu mugo* or medicine man, the worker in white magic, always conducted his business openly and by day, the *murogi* or worker in black magic and witchcraft worked secretly and usually by night. He worked in part by the actual use of poisons, skilfully administered, but for the most part he worked by the clever use of the psychology

49

of fear, which owed its power to the same absolute belief in magic that made it possible for the medicine man to do so much good. A worker in black magic would often prepare his evil charms of many noxious and 'unclean' materials and then, in the dead of night, place them in gazelle horns and other such containers around the hut of the person against whom he was working, or in the thatch. When the victim of such magical attacks discovered these things his fear was so great that in some cases death actually ensued as the direct result of fear. Or again the worker in black magic would obtain something that was a part of his intended victim, parings from his toe nails, or hair shaved from his head, or spittle from his mouth, and would then make black magic with such things and say evil spells over them. He would then let it be known that this had been done, not by an open and direct statement to the victim, but by insinuation and rumour, knowing that in due course the victim would hear of it.

So great was the belief in the powers of such black magic that the victim would be sure that he was doomed and, unless he could very speedily find the right counteracting white magic, he too might die of fear. Since any unaccountable sudden death was nearly always attributed by the Kikuyu to 'black magic', the belief in the powers of this evil practice were constantly being reinforced by events that in reality had a purely natural explanation. There can be little doubt that from time to time the black magic worker augmented his use of spells and charms by the actual administration of poison. Thus the discovery of a black magic charm by someone's hut or the news that an evil spell had been pronounced against a particular person was sometimes immediately followed by his death not, in this case, from fear, but from poison. These circumstances only enhanced the reputation of the black-magic worker since it was thought that he was capable of killing by his magic alone.

Although the family of some person who had died suddenly might suspect that the death had been caused by black magic administered at the behest of some enemy, it was rarely indeed that this could be proved, for no worker in black magic would ever openly admit to such an activity, nor would the person who had invoked his aid reveal him. On the very rare occasions when a case could be proved, a *murogi* or black-magic worker would be put to death as someone wholly anti-social, but the majority of such people continued their nefarious practices unhindered because nothing could be proved against them.

Quite apart from the practice of magic, both black and white, there was, of course, an implicit belief in magic and especially harmful magic that emanated from ordinary people either voluntarily or involuntarily. For example, some people had the misfortune to be born with an 'evil eye', so that if they looked upon other people's cattle or children or crops they would unwittingly cause them to die, or to wilt or at least grow thin and weak. If a person came to be aware that he suffered from this supernatural power, he would take infinite care never to stare at anyone's child, or at any person's flocks, for fear of being accused of causing wilful harm. If he could not avoid looking at such things, as when he was visiting in someone else's home, he would take steps to negate any unwitting harm that he might do by spitting at or in the direction of the things he looked upon, or by pointing at them with the thumb between the fore and middle fingers, acts which would at once stop the evil eye from working. Or again any person might inadvertently invoke natural evil powers by undue praise, and so no one would ever sing high praises of someone else's favourite bull or child for fear that by doing so he might bring disaster upon it.

It was this absolute fear of magic powers that was the foundation stone of all Kikuyu ceremonies of oath taking, and in consequence the taking of a solemn oath was an act never lightly undertaken, and once sworn, its effect upon the taker was very great. While no one was required to take an oath before giving evidence in judicial proceedings that he would 'speak the truth, the whole truth, and nothing but the truth' as we do in our courts, the administration of an oath was the chief way in which a dispute was settled if the court which was trying the case had failed, as it sometimes did, to come to a satisfactory verdict.

So skilled were Kikuyu judges in getting at the truth in a dispute, due chiefly to the fact that they were not bound by our British 'laws of evidence', that it but seldom happened that a decision was given which one or other party to the dispute knew in his heart was a miscarriage of justice. In such a case the aggrieved person had the right to demand that both he and the other party to the suit should be allowed by the court to take the *githathi* oath to settle the matter.

The court would then give its consent and fix a day upon which both parties should appear before them for a solemn oath-taking ceremony. Such a date was always fixed some weeks ahead to give both parties *and their families* time to consider carefully upon the wisdom or otherwise of having recourse to such a dangerous procedure; dangerous because, if proceeded with, the supernatural forces which would be invoked would certainly intervene to cause the death of one or more members of the family of the party who perjured himself. It was only very rarely that the two litigants did, in fact, take such an oath and then only if—as sometimes happened—each was absolutely sure that his claim was a true one, and even then only if the issue was of such importance that the risk of the supernatural forces deciding against one were worth it, not only for the individual, but from the point of view of the whole family.

As soon as a matter in dispute had reached a point where one or other litigant had decided to ask for the right to take an oath with his opponent, the families of both parties

52

would take a hand. The family of the man who had demanded the oath-taking ceremony would have to be wholly satisfied that his claim was true and that if he swore the solemn *githathi* oath to this effect he could do so with a clear conscience and with no risk. Similarly, the family of the party who had been awarded the decision by the court— which decision had caused the other party to demand an oath ceremony—would at once interview him and make him tell them the truth. Often, if he knew that he had won his case on false evidence, he himself would go to the court and decline to take the oath and ask the court to reverse the decision they had given, or else he would be forced to take such a step by the members of his family. For if he persisted and perjured himself at a *githathi* oath ceremony, the super-natural powers residing in the *githathi* stone might exact their punishment, not by causing the death of the individual, but rather of his father or his wife or his brother.

On the rare occasions when both parties believed that truth was on their side, the oath-taking ceremony would be proceeded with. The oath-stone was usually a stone with seven holes in it, symbolizing at one and the same time firstly, the seven apertures of the human body (the two ears, the two nostrils, the mouth, the anus, and the genital opening); secondly, the evil or unlucky number seven. The oath-stone was set upon a very special plant having seven branches together forming a platform upon which the stone could be set, and seven sticks of another plant were used as well. The ceremony must take place in public, in daylight, and with as many witnesses as possible. It would take too long and involve too much of an anthropo-logical dissertation to describe the whole details of such an oath-taking ceremony here, but briefly each party was called upon to insert one of the seven sticks seven times in each of the seven apertures, while at the same time solemnly declaring that if the claim he had made before the court, and which he had to repeat at the oath ceremony was false, he called upon the oath-stone to kill him and members of his family.

But this was not all; the parties who had taken such an oath were then debarred from any act of sexual intercourse with their wives, as were all the closely related adult members of the family for a period of seven planting seasons, or three and a half years, while all their male stock of cattle, goats, and sheep had to be castrated and prevented from acts of propagation for the same period.

It was implicitly believed that before this period of seven seasons had elapsed, the *githathi* stone would exert the power to kill; the family of the perjurer was indicated by the first death occurring within this period, and the court would then either confirm its award or reverse it as the case might be. Not only so, but as soon as one death had occurred, and before the effects of perjury caused further deaths within the three and a half year period, the family of the guilty party would take steps to be cleansed from the power of the oath, thereby admitting that their family was in the wrong. It will be seen from the above that for the Kikuyu an oath-taking ceremony according to native law and custom was: (*a*) one which could not be entered into lightly; (*b*) should be taken voluntarily and with the approval of the rest of the family; (*c*) had to be administered in public and in front of many witnesses.

Oath-taking ceremonies did not, of course, always derive from litigation. There were occasions when an oath-taking ceremony would be taken by representatives of two 'ridges', undertaken on pain of death from supernatural causes, to bring an end to some internecine feud between the two groups. Or an oath might be administered to a man suspected of black magic and who claimed to be wholly innocent, and whereby he swore that if he was not in fact innocent, he was prepared for supernatural powers to cause his death or the death of members of his family.

An oath-taking ceremony could even be taken, and was,

in fact, sometimes taken, between representatives of the Kikuyu tribe and their traditional enemies the Masai, whereby both tribes were bound for a period of seven planting seasons, or for multiples of seven seasons, not to engage in hostilities, warfare, or raiding activities. The administration of a solemn oath, moreover, was not always upon a *githathi* or oath-stone. Other objects could be used, many variations of oath ceremonies existed, but all had certain things in common. All involved the number seven, all invoked supernatural penalties, either for perjury or for breaking the promises made under such an oath.

As everyone knows, the Mau Mau leaders have made great use of the fear underlying an oath ceremony to carry out their evil campaign. We shall also see how, as the movement grew from its small beginning, it violated more and more the rules governing oath taking and so grew into something which was wholly contrary to established native law and custom.

PART TWO

The Kikuyu Today and the Mau Mau Movement

VII

THE COMING OF THE EUROPEAN

The earliest contacts between Europeans and the Kikuyu tribe were made with the Kikuyu of the Kiambu district, which by reason of its geographical position lay nearest to the great caravan routes running up to Uganda. At first the contacts consisted of meetings outside Kikuyu country proper, and were confined to trading operations in which the Kikuyu brought in vast quantities of grain, beans, and sweet potatoes to the caravans which were halted at the springs of Ngongo Bagas below the Ngong Hills. This place was outside the forest fringe which separated the grassy plains of Masai land from the Kikuyu agricultural area, but which ranked as Kikuyu country and contained many fortified villages.

By the time the caravans had reached Ngongo Bagas, their supplies of food for the porters were often running short and the next stage of the long journey would be mainly through the Masai country of the Great Rift Valley, where there was no agricultural produce. The opportunity, therefore, to revictual the caravans by bartering cloth, wire, and beads for corn and beans from the Kikuyu was always taken. The Kikuyu in those days were very greatly feared; a few earlier purely Arab caravans that had tried to penetrate Kikuyu land had been wiped out and the Arab headmen, who accompanied all the early European caravans as guides and interpreters, always advised against any attempt to take a short cut by going through Kikuyu territory.

In 1890, however, the British East Africa Company decided to set up a post within Kikuyu territory, at Dago-reti, a post which was built by Captain (later Lord)

57

Lugard and Mr. George Wilson. This station of the Company's was twice attacked and destroyed by the Kikuyu in eighteen months and then a stronger fort was built at a better situation, four miles farther into Kikuyu territory at Fort Smith. In 1892 there was severe fighting with the Kikuyu round Fort Smith and again in 1893, but a little later peace treaties were made and the relations between the Kikuyu and the British improved.

The engineers surveying the line for the Uganda Railway had helped in the fighting against the Kikuyu at this time and were among the earliest white men to make contact with the tribe. An early traveller who was probably the first to make peaceful contact with the Kikuyu of Nyeri district was Professor J. W. Gregory, who had passed through Fort Smith on his way to study the geology of the Great Rift Valley and Mount Kenya in 1893. It is tempting to turn this chapter into a brief historical account of the early contacts between the British and Kikuyu, but I must not do so as it is outside the scope of this book.

The coming of the first Europeans of the British East Africa Company to Kikuyu land, and especially to the Kiambu district, was followed by the arrival of Christian missions, of which the first were the Church of Scotland Mission which established a station at Thogoto; the Church Missionary Society, which started work at Kabete; and the Catholic White Fathers, who placed their first mission to the Kikuyu at St. Austin's, not far from where Nairobi now stands. All these first three mission stations were in the Kiambu district of Kikuyu and their positions are not without significance, for it will readily be realized that the sites chosen for such mission work were in the middle of the Kikuyu people whom the missionaries wished to evangelize and not on the extreme outskirts of their country.

These early missionaries to the Kikuyu did not find that the task of bringing Christianity to these people was an easy one. At first, naturally, the difficulty of language had to be overcome, but even when the missionaries had begun to be able to speak Kikuyu, it was not easy to persuade the people to abandon their own highly organized religious beliefs for those of Christianity. In addition to preaching the Gospel, the missionaries provided medical services, either by way of small hospitals or of dispensaries, and it was not long before many more Kikuyu were taking advantage of these facilities than of the Christian teaching. The missions, too, instituted schools at which their adherents—who to start with were mainly youths—could learn to read and write. Gradually and slowly the work of the missionaries grew and the number of stations increased and spread throughout the land.

Among the reasons for the early hostility to the work of the missions was the fact that once a youth had become a Christian he would refuse to participate in what he had been taught were heathen sacrifices, while on the other hand many Kikuyu ceremonies of religious worship and sacrifice to the ancestral spirits were invalid unless all the male members of the family were present. Fathers, therefore, strongly resented the wish of some of the young men to join the missions and there were many cases where a young man lost all his inheritance and was disowned on becoming a Christian. Once he had been so disowned, his absence from an act of family worship and sacrifice did not matter any more.

From the earliest days of contact with the white man, the Kikuyu, like other natives all over Africa, had been both mystified and highly intrigued by the white man's way of communicating with another far away by writing and by being able to read the writing of some other person. The desire to master this strange practice certainly played its part in bringing men and boys to the missions, and though many of them having come to the mission for this reason went on to be truly persuaded of the goodness of the Christian religion, there were always a few who nominally professed Christianity when at heart they did not approve or believe in it, simply because it was the password to learning the arts of reading and writing.

As time went on and as the number of mission stations extended all over Kikuyu country, the educational aspect of the mission work loomed largest. Government, which by then had taken over the administration from the old Company, thought it was better to leave the education of the Kikuyu to the missions, while the missionaries were always anxious to teach more and more Kikuyu how to read and write so that by reading for themselves they could personally study the Scriptures, which were fast being translated into the Kikuyu tongue.

The danger of this policy, and one to which neither Government nor missionaries seemed to be alive, was the danger—which had always been present—that many in their desire for this type of 'education' would temporarily and at least outwardly become adherents of Christianity for the sake of the learning which they could get at the mission schools, while they did not accept the Christian doctrine or have any intention of really trying to live up to Christian standards of morality, honesty, and codes of behaviour. At the same time, many of these young men— and as time went on young women too—learned enough to make them cease to have real faith in their own Kikuyu religious beliefs and practices, so that a body of people sprang into being who had abandoned one faith without accepting another in its place and who were thus without any real guiding principles in their lives.

At first, too, the number of Kikuyu attending the mission schools, and the classes for religious instruction at the missions, were so small that the missionaries themselves were able to know each member of their flock very intimately and were able to give them an immense amount of personal training. This more than made up for the fact that these people were in many cases no longer taking any part in the processes of 'education' in the Kikuyu sense and which we have already outlined in an earlier chapter. But as the number attending mission schools grew, so did it become more and more impossible for any individual training and instruction to be given. The teaching given at the missions became, inevitably, more and more a matter of the type of secular education that is given in a classroom combined with religious instruction given to large numbers of 'catechumens' prior to their admittance to the sacrament of baptism.

It should not be thought that the missionaries were entirely to blame; they were few in number and would very much have preferred to have been able to give personal instruction to a smaller number and to have been sure that each and every adherent really would be worthy to be called a Christian. Nearly all of the missionaries were only too painfully aware of the many 'black sheep' among their flock who were bringing Christianity and missionary teaching into ill repute, but Government was not ready to take upon itself the burden of secular education and was only too thankful to let the missionary societies carry on, even at the expense of the better carrying out of their real duties, the teaching of the Gospel of Christ.

It is, I think, of the utmost significance today that the leaders and also the followers of such movements as the Mau Mau are not drawn from those who are truly Christian, nor yet from those who have remained true to the old Kikuyu religion and who are horrified by the methods of Mau Mau and of its teaching. They are drawn rather from the thousands of so-called Christians, nominally, but only nominally, adherents of one or other of the Christian missions, or from the many thousands of others who belong to the separatist Kikuyu churches of which we shall have more to say in another chapter. The Kikuyu pastors, church elders, and genuine adherents of the various Christian missions have been unanimous in their resistance to Mau

61

Mau and are suffering persecution and even death rather than have anything to do with it, as are the out and out followers of the old Kikuyu and so-called 'pagan' religion.

When the British Government took over the administration of what is now Kenya (formerly called the British East African Protectorate), a number of administrative centres were set up in Kikuyu country the chief of which were the *Bomas* at Kiambu, Fort Hall, and Nyeri, as the administrative centres of these three well-established divisions of the older Kikuyu territorial organization. While the administration laid it down that in such matters as trials for murder and other serious offences in future the British administrator would have the sole judicial authority, there was little if any interference at first with any of the ordinary Kikuyu methods of justice or administration, save that government 'chiefs' and headmen were appointed, whose duties included the helping of the government authorities to collect poll tax and to report on all that was being done in their areas.

The administrative officers themselves spent very long periods on foot safaris through their districts, camping at or near the villages of 'chiefs' and making most valuable personal contacts not only with the 'chiefs' but with members of the population, giving them friendship, giving valuable advice and winning the confidence of the masses. Gradually the people came to look upon these British officers as their helpers as well as their friends, and it became more and more recognized that the white man was there to assist and not to oppress, and for a time Government or *serekali* as the Africans call it was a symbol of all that was good.

But, alas, as time went on things changed; the duties of administrative officers became more and more involved in paper work in the office and there was less and less time for the administrator to spend days on end on foot safaris in his

62

district, getting to know the people and earning their confidence as his predecessors had done. Instead, more and more of the duties of the government officer were delegated to educated Kikuyu clerks and headmen, many of whom were regrettably far from scrupulous or honest in their dealings with their fellow Kikuyu, but rather took advantage of their position of authority for self-aggrandizement. Gradually, for many, the word *serekali* or Government ceased to be synonymous with good and honest dealings. Nor was the reputation of Government as an organization enhanced by the fluctuating policies of successive holders of administrative posts. An officer would express hopes or sometimes even, rashly, make actual promises that this or that would be done in the district and his successor would reverse the policy or break what had been regarded as promises (even if sometimes they had not really been promises at all, but only 'pious hopes') and many Kikuyu began to doubt whether Government could really be trusted at all.

To make matters worse, the growing need for the administrative officer to spend the greater part of his time in his office meant that more and more had he to rely upon calling in his 'chiefs' and headmen and giving them instructions and directives as to policy, leaving it to them to call meetings in their areas to pass on the government's instructions. All too often the meaning of the message was woefully altered by the time it reached the masses. Things that the District Commissioner had said in Swahili to his chiefs 'that he would try to do', reached the people, when addressed in the vernacular by the chiefs and headmen, as specific undertakings, and when what were believed to be promises were not fulfilled, 'Government' was blamed for 'bad faith', while in fact since no promise had been given, it could not have been broken.

The coming of missionaries and administrators was followed about 1902 by the arrival of the first settlers, men who came to make their homes in the Protectorate to settle in the fullest meaning of the word, the vast majority of whom were not in the least 'exploiters', but who came to live among and to help in the uplifting of the Africans, whom they thought of as 'poor ignorant savages'. Naturally these men and their wives wanted land, land which they could call their own, where they could build their homes and rear their families. They saw the nearly empty country, which had once been part of the 'vast garden' described by the early travellers in the previous century, and which had become so nearly empty for the tragic reasons that we have already summarized in an earlier chapter.

This land was rich and fertile, it was at a high altitude where the effects of being on the equator were counter-balanced by the height and where the climate was therefore most agreeable. Moreover, the early 'gardens' of the people who had been in charge of stations like Fort Smith had proved that this was a land where nearly every English crop could grow, as well as many others that would not thrive in Britain; not unnaturally they asked that some of this land be alienated to them for farming. Many could even be said to have come out at the invitation of Government, for it was part of the policy to encourage settlers.

It was a widely held belief among the British—one might almost say universally held—that amongst the Bantu, land was not held as property, that all an African member of a tribe had to do was to go into any uncultivated part of the tribal lands and proceed to clear it and plant his crops on it and build his home, and that none would say him nay. The idea that there was any part of Africa where land was privately owned, where in fact it had actually been purchased, was unthought of. A considerable portion of the Kiambu district of Kikuyu land was sparsely occupied and it was genuinely thought and believed by Government and would-be settlers alike that no hardship would be caused if the few who were on this land were told that they could either remain as labourers for the farmer who was being allocated the land, or else if they preferred, move off and settle somewhere else.

Thus quite considerable portions of the south-eastern corner of the Kiambu division of Kikuyu land were alienated, mostly on a freehold basis, but sometimes on a long lease from the Crown. All the native land came to be called Crown Land and was even designated as such by Ordinance. In practically every case payments were made to the Kikuyu who were then living on the land that was alienated. Attempts were also made to explain that these payments were for 'purchase', while at other times the payments were simply called compensation for disturbance. The British were wholly unaware that from the point of view of Kikuyu law these payments did not and could not ever rank as purchase of the land; at best they could only rank as payments for the right to cultivate, subject always to the real owner being allowed—at some future date—to evict the occupier.

By Kikuyu law these transactions could not be regarded as transferring ownership for many reasons, a few of which may be reiterated. (a) No transaction for the transfer of the *ownership* of land to a person of another tribe could take place unless first of all the two parties had been linked by a ceremony of mutual adoption or *guciarana*; (b) no final transfer of ownership could be completed unless the boundaries of the land so sold were marked out in the presence of witnesses and to the accompaniment of a religious ceremony; (c) no sale of land was valid unless other members of the landowning family had been given a 'first refusal', neither was it valid without the sanction of all the members of the land-owning family. And so from the Kikuyu point of view none of the rights acquired in Kikuyu lands by the white settlers were considered as vesting ownership in the new-comers, while from the point of view of British law, and the

65

country was now administered by the British, the transactions were wholly valid and had been made in absolute good faith.

It must here be stated clearly that only a *very small proportion* of Kikuyu land relative to the whole was alienated to white settlers, and that hundreds of thousands of Kikuyu families in Nyeri, Fort Hall, and even in the Kiambu division (where most of the alienation took place), never lost one single square inch of their land property. Unfortunately, however, the relatively small area that was alienated was all private property and it was sufficiently large to leave a not inconsiderable number of Kikuyu families landless.

It is necessary here to make quite sure that my meaning is clear when I say *landless*. At the time of the land alienation, so far as it affected the Kikuyu (and it must be understood that I am only dealing with what was truly Kikuyu land), there were many other parts of Kikuyu territory, and especially so in the Kiambu division itself, which were not alienated and which at that time were not carrying a very large population.

The Kikuyu who were in residence on the land that was alienated in all good faith were, therefore, able at the time to go to the owners of this other land and by agreement with them become *ahoi* under the tenant system of the Kikuyu, with rights of cultivation and the right to build a home. In other words they were *able to find land to occupy and live on* without difficulty, but since they were now tenants and this land belonged to others, they could not pass it on to their children and their children's children. They were tenants, where formerly they had been land-owners with full property rights in land of their own, and all the advantages (including the ability to have tenants of their own) which ownership gave.

In my boyhood days, at the time of the alienations, I do not think that any Kikuyu who had been dispossessed of

66

his land to make room for European settlers ever believed that it was more than a temporary affair. It was not until just after the First World War that members of Kikuyu land-owning families, who had moved back to friends and relatives in the Fort Hall and Nyeri districts at the time of the four great disasters, began to return to Kiambu. They then found in the case of those parts of the Kiambu division where alienation had taken place, that the European farmers claimed the land as their own private property.

By this time, of course, quite a few Kikuyu had received a fair measure of education in our English sense, one or two had been to England and returned, and thousands had been away from their homes helping to fight the common enemy in what had been German East Africa, as members of the Carrier Corps. There was therefore a nucleus of men —mostly fairly young men—who had begun to see further than the narrow confines of their home lands, who had begun to think—not always clearly and logically—about the problems of their people, and so in 1922 there was born the first Kikuyu political organization, the Kikuyu Central Association, led by a band of young men fired with immense patriotism and armed with a little learning, who made the first slogan of their party 'We must be given back the lands which the white man has stolen from us.'

We shall examine the development of the Association in more detail in a later chapter and see how it gradually led up to the present Mau Mau movement.

VIII

CHANGES IN THE PRESENT CENTURY

As we have already seen, at the end of the last century
Kikuyu customs relating to the land were very highly organized, particularly in the Kiambu area, or that part of the
Kikuyu country that lay south of the Chania River. We
have also seen that it was in this area that the effects of the
four major catastrophies were most pronounced, so that, by
1902, the population actually resident on the land was
greatly reduced, especially in certain areas.

We have seen, too, that when members of the Kikuyu
land-owning families whose land had been alienated to
European farmers (in all good faith) started moving back,
and found that their own land was occupied by European
farmers, they were content, for the time being, to become
tenants or *ahoi* on the estates of other land-owning families,
which at that time, were not overcrowded.

Gradually, as the population increased, and also as the
effects of the introduction and spread of European civilization and economy began to be more apparent, a number of
events took place which have a bearing on the problem of
today.

In the first place, the more educated Kikuyu, becoming
aware that European farmers claimed the complete ownership of the lands they occupied by virtue of title deeds, began
to demand that '*Tidlydee*', as title deeds were called, should
be granted to such Kikuyu as still actually owned land.
This demand came from a genuine fear—if one without
foundation—that as the European population increased,
still more land would be alienated for European farms. Nor
was this fear allayed by the fact that they were refused such
title deeds, on the grounds that all Kikuyu land ranked as

'Crown Land' under the Crown Lands Ordinance, and that the Kikuyu were, in effect, only tenants at will of the Crown.

The majority of Government officials were still wholly unaware (and when informed, usually sceptical) of the fact that the Kikuyu system of land tenure, in the Kiambu area, was on the basis of ownership of estates with well-marked boundaries. It was still believed that the land was held communally by all members of the tribe, and that any person could build huts and cultivate any piece of land, wherever he chose, provided it was not already being used by someone else. This belief was probably not dispelled until 1929, after the report of the Kikuyu Land Inquiry Committee, of which I was a member. Since this report was not as widely read as it might have been, the old idea continued in the minds of many Europeans.

The failure to grant title deeds for land actually owned caused widespread discontent and disappointment. It must, however, be admitted that it would have been exceedingly difficult to grant this request, even if it had been understood at the time that it was entirely reasonable, because such title deeds could not be granted without a proper survey, and there were not enough surveyors available to undertake the task.

Another trend which had far-reaching effects became apparent about this time. A number of Kikuyu had become very wealthy, and these people sought every opportunity to buy land from others in less fortunate circumstances, tempting them to part with their land by offering very high prices. These transfers of land rights among the Kikuyu themselves, further increased the numbers of those without land of their own.

A number of unscrupulous people also began to file suits in the courts of the British administration, claiming land that was not theirs, hoping that the failure of the magistrates to understand fully the intricacies of the Kikuyu land system might enable them to win their cases, even if their claims were wholly unjust. In the early days, as we have seen, there was a strong safeguard against such miscarriages of justice, because, if the court made a wrong decision, the aggrieved party could demand an oath-taking ceremony, and, if his cause was just, he would be backed by his family. On the other hand, the person who had won the case by means of false testimony would not be allowed by his family to participate in such a ceremony for fear of the consequences, not only to himself, but to other members of his family.

After the coming of the Europeans, however, there were a number of Kikuyu with just enough education and with a sufficient disbelief in their own ancient customs to be willing to take the risk of perjury in an oath-stone ceremony, since they no longer really believed in punishment by the supernatural powers. Thus there began an era of ever-increasing numbers of law suits concerning land tenure; an era which continues until the present time, with perjury as a frequent feature.

Yet another factor began to make its appearance, further to increase the discontent over land. Many of the more educated younger men, who belonged to families who did not actually own land, had received enough education to wish to build good, clean houses for themselves and their families instead of the old-style Kikuyu huts.

Some of these young men were members of the families whose land had been alienated to the Europeans; some were members of families who had moved into the Kiambu district many generations before, as *ahoi*, or tenants, and who could not return to their original homes and claim their own land as, by this time, it was already over-populated; others were victims of excessive land purchase by wealthy Kikuyu.

All of these young men, however, had one thing in common: they were land-less and they wanted to build good permanent homes, not old-style timber, or mud and wattle, huts. As *ahoi*, they were not allowed by the land-owners to build such houses, since the landlords argued, reasonably enough, that once a tenant had built such a house, it would be very difficult indeed to evict him.

It might be supposed that these young men would have been able to buy various pieces of land that were offered for sale from time to time, and in a few cases they did so. For the most part, however, they were unable to compete against the high prices being offered by the wealthy for any available land. It was the young men who found themselves in these circumstances who became the leaders of those who were always demanding of Government that the land 'stolen' from the Kikuyu for European farms should be returned, or else, that land in other parts of the country should be given to them in compensation.

In 1932 a Royal Commission, known as the Carter Land Commission, was appointed to inquire into the question of native lands, as Government had realized, by then, that there were genuine grievances and cases of hardship throughout the Colony, especially among the Kikuyu.

Unfortunately the Kikuyu, ill-advised by the leaders of the Kikuyu Central Association, put such outrageous claims before the Commission that many just claims were set aside and the whole matter was obscured. Had this not occurred, it is likely that the recommendations of the Commission would have taken a more generous form. As it was, the Commission recognized that the Kikuyu, especially of the Kiambu division, had lost a considerable amount of land and compensation was recommended, as well as the provision of certain new land for Kikuyu settlement. These recommendations, moreover, were implemented. Unfortunately some of the land thus made available—although it was not part of the Kikuyu Reserve as then demarcated—was land which the Kikuyu claimed to have been theirs originally.

71

This is not the place in which to discuss in detail the recommendations of the Carter Land Commission, which were accepted by Government as a final settlement of all Kikuyu land claims. It must suffice to say that the Kikuyu were very far from satisfied. Everyone who knows the Kikuyu country as it is today must admit that the land is very overcrowded, with the exception of certain small areas in the Nyeri district; it is carrying an agricultural population at a density which makes it very difficult for the people to grow enough food, even for subsistence, especially in view of the existing methods of farming.

But the Kikuyu of today who live in the native land units are not content merely to grow enough for subsistence. They want to improve their conditions of living, wear better clothes, educate their children and do many other things that are manifestly impossible for the majority to achieve, since the present overcrowded state of the land means that most people only have a very small acreage at their disposal.

Tens of thousands of Kikuyu are also living as squatters on European farms up-country, where, like the *ahoi* in Kikuyu land itself, they are only tenants, with no rights of property, and liable to eviction at any time, though of course, with due notice. But the clause concerning 'due notice' is of little comfort to a family when it knows that if it is evicted, it will be very nearly impossible to find anywhere else to move, where there will be enough land available to live on.

The policy of the Forest Department to encourage 'forest squatters' has done something to alleviate the problem temporarily, and there are now thousands of Kikuyu families who live and have their homes—albeit temporary homes—in the forest reserves, supplying labour for afforestation and other forestry work. It can truthfully be said that most of these families like living as forest squatters and are reasonably content. But among them, too, young men are growing up who are restless because they know there is no security, not any prospect of owning part of the land themselves.

Some Kikuyu families have tried to find an answer to these problems by going to live in the lands of other tribes. There are a good many today who have persuaded Masai families to adopt them and who are living and practising agriculture in certain parts of Masai land. There are others who have gone as far afield as the Kisii Reserve in Nyanza Province, and there have bought land from the Kisii who are still not very overcrowded. Many, too, have migrated to Tanganyiki territory in search of land there.

Yet another factor connected with the problem of Kikuyu land is that which affects the many urban Kikuyu. There are really very few Kikuyu who are truly city-dwellers, although thousands are to be found living in towns like Nairobi, Nakuru, Mombasa, and Kisumu, and also as far as Arusha in Tanganyika Territory. The vast majority of these Kikuyu are not urban in the strict sense of the term; they are merely town-dwellers in that their work lies in the towns and cities, but they nearly all retain a home in the native lands, either as land-owners if they are lucky, or as tenants. With very few exceptions, they intend to live on the land when they retire.

Under conditions as they are now, this is essential, for few of them own any land, or even a house in the towns, and when their days of earning are finished they will have to leave. In nearly all cases there is no such thing as a pension to look forward to when employment comes to an end, nor is there any hope, on present scales of salary, of saving enough to live on in their old age. Therefore, if they did not retain a piece of land in the native land units—either as landlords or as tenants—they could only look forward to an old age of starvation, with nowhere to live. Naturally, the fact that the thousands of urban Kikuyu have holdings in the native lands does not help to alleviate the overcrowding of those who must always live there and make their living as agriculturalists.

We must turn now from the land problems of the Kikuyu to other aspects of Kikuyu life which have altered very considerably during the last fifty years. We have already briefly examined the marriage customs, as ordained by Kikuyu tribal law and custom. Marriage in olden days was stabilized by the payment of 'marriage insurance'. The young Kikuyu married man lived near to his family home, his wife's people were not far away, and the families of both parties were able to intervene and assist if there seemed any likelihood of the marriage breaking up. Marriage insurance, moreover, was paid in the form of goats and sheep and sometimes cattle (mainly contributed by the family of the young man and not by the young man himself). Such stock received by the bride's family could not be sold or otherwise disposed of (even for payment of marriage insurance for a son of the family), until such time as it became apparent that the marriage would not break down.

The coming of European civilization, the European economic system, and the Christian religion, have all contributed to change this arrangement. Nowadays, although the old custom of paying *ruracio* or marriage insurance is still retained in form, it has completely lost its former meaning; it is no longer a safeguard for marriage and has become a terrible burden on the young people.

In the first place, a system of economy based on money has come into existence, and, since few Kikuyu families have enough land on which to graze many goats and sheep, the marriage insurance payments are now often made in hard cash. Such cash payments having been made, it is not at all easy for the bride's family to resist the temptation to spend the money forthwith, to buy things which they need such as food or clothes, or perhaps even a plough or a motor-car. And so, what used to be an insurance for the marriage, and could be returned, together with all the computed

74

offspring (when it was paid in goats and sheep), in the event of the marriage breaking up, became more and more a payment for the 'purchase' of a wife.

Secondly, whereas, in the past, the family of the young man helped to pay the marriage insurance, or almost all of it, it has now become more and more necessary for the young man to save money from his own earnings until he has about £100, in order to enable him to make the required payment to the bride's family. Not infrequently, a young man who is anxious to hasten his wedding day borrows money to make up the necessary amount, and then finds himself in debt for years to come, because he has not taken into account the fact that when he is married his living expenses will be greatly increased and he will be unable to save enough to pay off the debt. Sometimes when hard-pressed by his creditors, if he owns land, he sells it in order to get out of his difficulties, and thus swells the land-less class who must be *ahoi* or tenants for the rest of their lives.

Again, under present-day conditions, instead of newly married couples living near their respective families, hundreds of young men go to work far from their homes and take their young brides with them. Their work may take them to the cities, or to up-country farms, but it nearly always takes them out of reach of the family influence. Under present-day conditions, too, it often happens that the difficulties which face a young married couple are much more serious than in the olden days, and the circumstances are far less conducive to a happy marriage, so that many of these marriages break up. The woman is far from her people, and if she leaves her husband she often does not return to her home, but may join the ever-increasing number of prostitutes in the towns or else make a semi-permanent liaison with some man to whom she is not married, either by native law and custom, or by the Christian ceremony, or by ordinary civil marriage.

The prostitute class, too, is swelled today by a number of girls who in olden days would have become second wives in a polygamous household, having failed to find a young man who wanted them as first and senior wife. Such girls not infrequently drift into the towns, either in search of temporary liaisons with men who will give them a good time, or in search of employment as an *ayah* or children's nurse in a European household. All too often, these girls eventually drift into the ranks of the prostitutes. It is not a happy picture.

I have indicated in an earlier chapter how the young men and women who had undergone initiation were allowed—and even encouraged—to indulge in a degree of familiarity, provided that full sexual intercourse did not take place. Under the new conditions, and the modified form of initiation which had come into existence, this old practice continued. But the young men and women were no longer held back by the fear of ostracism by members of the age group if they contravened custom. In consequence, the number of girls who became pregnant before marriage began to increase steadily. Moreover, they had frequently had affairs with so many different young men that they had no idea who was the father of the coming child, and there were thus many unmarried mothers. This state of affairs has become increasingly serious yearly.

Under conditions as they are today among the Kikuyu, young boys and girls get little of the education in behaviour, native law and custom, and character training that were all part of the organized tribal educational system. The vast majority of the boys and girls go to school; to mission schools, to government schools, and to independent schools. In all of these, owing to the shortage of fully trained teachers, and of teachers for whom their profession is a real vocation, the classes are very large. The emphasis is placed on the pupils acquiring enough book knowledge to pass examinations, so that there is all too little real education

76

in preparation for becoming adult members of the community.

It should perhaps be stressed that the Kikuyu thirst for 'education' is insatiable. For them, the key to better salaries, a higher earning capacity, and a better chance to satisfy their needs, lies in education.

Among ourselves, a large part of the character and moral training of our children is considered to be among the normal duties of the parents—and long may it remain so. There are, too, many Kikuyu parents, especially among the genuine Christians and among those who still retain faith in their ancient beliefs who try to train their children to become fit members of the adult community. But there are countless other Kikuyu children today for whom 'education' means only book learning and who are growing up without any real preparation for good citizenship and the responsibilities of modern life. On this failure of the education system that we have introduced, in place of the old tribal one, a heavy responsibility for the troubles of today must rest.

IX

THE BREAKDOWN OF TRIBAL CUSTOMS

In the days of my boyhood, when I lived in the Kikuyu
Reserve, thieving was to all intents and purposes unknown,
either from fellow Kikuyu or from members of other tribes
or races, if they were living in the country as accepted
neighbours. Raiding the Masai for cattle, sheep, and goats
was not accounted as stealing. It was an act of war against
the traditional enemy (except at such times as there was a
state of peace between the two tribes) and was in quite a
different category.

The absence of thieving was not due to the fear of punishment by man or by the native courts, but due to the fact that
'it was not done' to steal and a person who was proved to be
a thief would be 'sent to Coventry' so effectively by his age-
group and banned from all social affairs, that his life would
not be worth living. Thieving was contrary to native law
and custom and anyone who deliberately went against this
rule was an outcast—a *njangiri*. There were, of course, a
certain number of Kikuyu who were thieves, but having
been ranked as *njangiri* they were outcasts and disinherited
and disowned by their families. In consequence, if such a
person was killed when caught red-handed, it did not rank
as murder or even manslaughter, any more than causing
the death of a raider from another tribe would rank as a
crime.

So long as tribal law and custom was respected, property
was safe, but with the breakdown of the old system following
the coming of European civilization, all this changed. The
age-group system, from being highly organized, became a
shadow of its former self. Initiation ceremonies of a very
curtailed type still take place in order that the boys and

girls may receive the 'outward and visible sign' that marks the transition from childhood to adult status. But the cohesion of the age-groups has gone. Whereas, in the past, all the members of a single age-group, in any given '*rugongo*' or ridge, were a close-knit body, meeting together regularly, dancing together on moonlight nights, and with their own chosen leaders, today, after the brief initiation ceremony which has replaced the age-old customs, all the members separate: some go off to work on far away farms, or in the towns, others return to school to continue their education. There is no longer any age-group loyalty, the members of the age-group within the various territorial areas never meet regularly and therefore the fear of exclusion from age group affairs has ceased to exert any power to control the action of the individual.

At the same time, the temptation to steal has increased a thousand fold. The needs of young men and women in the olden days were small, and they were met without difficulty by their own families. Young men, seeking to enhance their reputation with the girls, did so by deeds of bravery, by excelling at dancing, by being such good organizers or speech-makers that they were chosen by their fellows as leaders. Today, a young man, after initiation, feels that in order to make an impression with the girls, he must dress well in European clothes, must have a bicycle with a pillion to take his girl friends for rides, and so on. As he very often cannot earn enough to fulfil this need for exhibitionism of the average courting male, the temptation to steal becomes measurably greater. Actual need and want, as distinct from exhibitionism, also plays a part; many young men, who go off in search of work in the towns and cities, find it hard to get a job and then the day comes when hunger or other needs provide a great temptation, an opportunity occurs, and the downward path has begun. The youth knows he should not steal, but the training against such an act has not been strong enough, while the moral support against

79

such conduct that membership of an active age-group organization would have given, is lacking.

In recent times (the last twelve years or so), a great effort has been made by some Kikuyu to try to revive age-group pride and cohesion. Those who were responsible for raising the funds for the Kenya Teachers College at Githunguri have used the age-groups for this purpose. But the lack of cohesion in the age-groups is so great that only a small proportion of the members have co-operated in the movement.

The same break-down of the age-group organizations and the collapse of respect for ancient law and custom is reflected in the drunkenness that is a common feature among the young people today. In olden days, intoxicating liquor was not consumed by young people save on very rare occasions, when perhaps a little was allowed to them by their elders. The drinking of native beer was the prerogative of the elders and the older married women, while drunkenness was only tolerated in people who were grandparents. Any young man who somehow managed to get enough alcohol to get drunk would have been so heavily punished by the members of his age-group, whom he had thus disgraced, that he would be unlikely to risk such a thing again.

Under native law and custom, as we have seen, law suits were heard by courts consisting of nine elders, assisted by such specialists as they might choose to call in, and the nature of the court which heard the evidence in a dispute depended upon whether it was a matter affecting members of a village, a 'fire-linked unit', or of a ridge. If the case was not successfully decided, the matter could either be 'put back in the fire again', i.e., an appeal made to a court higher up the scale, or there could be recourse to the oath-stone procedure. It was customary that both parties to a law suit should pay *an identical* fee to the court before proceedings started, a fee, moreover, that was not recoverable.

80

Neither could the party that won the suit claim the fee he had paid, as part of his costs. With the introduction of European legal procedure and the setting up of native tribunals and appeal courts under the British administration, the complainant pays a fee when he lodges his suit, but the defendant pays nothing, unless he loses the case, in which case the fee paid by the plaintiff can be claimed as part of the costs. I believe that it was this idea, which is so much at variance with old Kikuyu custom, which was first responsible for the appearance of bribery in Kikuyu courts. The defendant in a case felt that if the plaintiff had paid a fee into court while he had not paid a similar fee, the elders might be prejudiced in favour of the plaintiff; therefore he would offer a ram, or some money, to the elders, in order to even things up. This of course could not be shown, by British custom, as a fee paid by the defendant and so it tended to become a 'gift' to the elders. The plaintiff sometimes felt that the defendant had made a 'gift' which was more valuable than the 'fee' he had paid, and so he would sometimes augment his 'fee' by a further 'gift'. This practice has become so widespread that the administration has had to take strong steps, on many occasions, against bribery, but it cannot truthfully be said that bribery has been stamped out. In fact, in one form or another it is one of the greatest evils in the native courts today, and probably one of the hardest to put a stop to.

I have said so much about how the break-down of age-old customs has led to the present unhappy state of affairs, that I fear I have been in danger of giving the impression that, whereas everything in the olden days was happy and rosy, the coming of the white man has brought nothing but discontent, dishonesty, and evil. To leave such an idea in the minds of any of my readers would be to give a very false picture and to conclude this chapter I will briefly summarize some of the many good results of the introduction of European civilization.

First and foremost on this list must come the improvement in health and hygiene, which of course has had its effect in the very rapid rise in the population. Hospitals and dispensaries and the teaching of better methods of hygiene to boys and girls, men and women, have been of the greatest possible blessing to the Kikuyu. Epidemics of smallpox, plague, and other such diseases may still break out, but they can never again result in the appalling high death-rate for which they were once responsible. Whereas the average Kikuyu woman has an easy delivery at childbirth, and needs little specialized medical attention in the case of a normal birth, abnormal births used to take a heavy toll of life. Nowadays, maternity hospitals all over Kikuyu country provide not only for lying-in patients, but also for pre-natal examination and advice and have proved a very great boon to the people, who gradually, yet very surely, have come to have great faith in our medical services.

The second major benefit conferred by the coming of our civilization is the banishing of the fear of famines—famines such as in the past killed off thousands of the tribe. Today, if serious drought results in the complete failure of a harvest in one part of Kenya, the administration arranges reliefs and the supply of foodstuffs from other less affected areas of East Africa or even from farther afield. Famine has been banished from the land.

Pax Britannica, too, has meant that the fear of a sudden night raid by warriors of the Masai tribe has gone, even for those living nearest to the Kikuyu-Masai boundary while it has, of course, also saved the Masai from similar attacks by warriors of the Kikuyu age-groups, who by no means let the Masai have things all their own way.

Vastly improved methods of agriculture have been learned from European settlers and from Government agricultural advisers, but for which the land now available to the Kikuyu could not support its present over-crowded population.

Many new types of food plants, too, have been introduced and play a very important part in Kikuyu economy—potatoes (known as English potatoes in contrast to the sweet potatoes of the Kikuyu), peas, many kinds of vegetables, improved high-yield strains of maize, and many fruits. Other agricultural products, too, which are of great importance as cash crops, have been introduced. Among those are black wattle, which is the foundation of the charcoal and the wattle-bark industries, as well as the primary source of fuel for Nairobi; pyrethrum, grown by a few Kikuyu, but still mainly a European crop; and flowers for the cut-flower market in the cities. All of these have provided the Kikuyu with considerable sources of income which were unknown before.

Improved strains of domestic animals have been introduced, cattle and sheep in particular (little has been done to improve native goats) and also fowls, all of which are very important to the Kikuyu economy of the present day.

Education as taught by us, although it has its drawbacks which I have already discussed, has also proved of immense value, in other respects, to the Kikuyu; not only in enabling him to get more highly paid work than he could do as an illiterate, but also because there has been a good deal of technical education, so that many Kikuyu are very competent masons, carpenters, builders, mechanics, etc.

Freedom of movement has come too, and a native of any tribe can go into the territory of any other tribe, thanks to *Pax Britannica*—trading, visiting, or on any other mission—without the smallest fear of personal attack.

The advantages that have accompanied the coming of the European are so numerous, and so important, that no thinking Kikuyu would ever dream of saying that he would like to go back to the 'good old days' of fifty years ago. Troubles and problems and grievances he has, worries of all kinds about his future, things he would like to have

83

altered or improved, but he has gained much more than he has lost, and if his progress is not too seriously retarded by such movements as Mau Mau, the future is full of hope.

Kikuyu country as it is today is vastly different from what it was in my boyhood days. Then, every Kikuyu lived in an old-style hut; now there are hundreds of good stone houses, thousands of good clean semi-permanent wattle and daub houses, with windows and decent furniture, and although there are also still hundreds of thousands of old-style unhygienic huts, these are disappearing faster and faster.

When I was a boy there was not a single shop in Kikuyu country, now there are hundreds of well-built stone shops, owned by Kikuyu merchants, where the housewife and the peasant farmer can buy soap, clothes, blankets, food stuffs, various medicines such as aspirin and other things they need.

When I was young, most Kikuyu were still dressed in old-style native leather clothes, with a few wearing blankets or dirty pieces of cotton cloth slung over their shoulders. Today, throughout Kikuyu country, there are Kikuyu tailors with sewing machines of their own, cutting out and making dresses, shirts, trousers, shorts, etc., for their innumerable customers.

No motor-vehicle existed when I was a boy, for white or black; now thousands of Kikuyu own lorries, buses, cars, and motor-bicycles. The sight of a camera, in the hands of a European trying to get a picture of the 'savages' to send to his family at home, often caused consternation. Today there are many Kikuyu with cameras of their own and very few Kikuyu houses without a picture of the wedding party or the latest baby hung upon the wall.

The surprising thing about the Kikuyu is not so much how little they have gained from European civilization, in the short space of fifty years, but how much they have absorbed and learned. It is probably because the speed of progress has been too rapid that it has made a part of the population unbalanced in their outlook and thus paved the way for movements like the Mau Mau, in the hands of an unscrupulous few.

X

KIKUYU POLITICAL MOVEMENTS

When the Kikuyu Central Association, or K.C.A., as it was known (and under which term I shall refer to it in this book), came into existence in 1922, with the expressed intention of finding a way to recover the 'lost lands' of the Kikuyu, it was an easy matter to gather together a large following, drawn particularly from the many members of the land-owning families who then had no land that they could call their own.

Some of these people were living as squatters on land which had formerly belonged to them, working for the new European estate owners. Others were scattered throughout the length and breadth of Kikuyu country, living as *ahoi* or tenants on other Kikuyus' estates. These estates, with the rapidly growing rate of increase in the population, were yearly becoming more congested, so that, more and more, tenants were evicted in favour of members of the family. Yet others moved out on to European farms farther afield, to become squatters and agricultural labourers.

Under the 'squatter' system a European land-owner signed an agreement with a Kikuyu family, whereby the head of the family was given the right to build a homestead and cultivate a portion of land and also to graze his own cattle, sheep, and goats on the European farm, provided that, in return, he and members of his family, resident with him, would work for the farmer at such times as called upon to do so, and for a small salary.

In the vast majority of cases the relationship between the farmer and his squatter labour was very good indeed; the farmer often provided a school and a paid teacher so that the children of the squatter families were able to get some education without having to go far from home. The squatters, moreover, usually had a much bigger acreage to cultivate and more space to graze their flocks and herds than they would have had as tenants in the very overcrowded Kikuyu lands. The system at first appeared to be working very satisfactorily, but there were certain inherent difficulties that became more and more apparent as time went on.

For one thing, the population of a Kikuyu family did not remain static, nor did the flocks and herds remain at a constant figure. Thus, when a European farmer protested that he had not bargained for a marked increase in the human and animal population of his farm, and that some must move, the Kikuyu frequently answered—and truthfully—that there was nowhere else for him and his family and stock to go to. He could not return with all his family to the overcrowded native lands because he had no hope of finding any Kikuyu land-owner who would accept a man with a large family and many domestic animals as a *muhoi*, or tenant; there was not room enough.

Similarly, the chances of being taken on as a squatter on some other European farm became yearly smaller and smaller, because the same sort of thing had been happening on nearly all the farms where there were Kikuyu squatters, so that most farmers had been trying to get rid of some of their squatters, not to take on more.

The K.C.A. leaders were also able, in the beginning, to enlist a great deal of support for their movement to 'get back the land', among families who had not lost any of their own land, but who were patriotically prepared to support their less fortunate tribesmen.

Not being very mature in political matters, the leaders of the K.C.A., in 1922, and during the next few years, did not realize that their best chance to achieve some redress would be to make out a well-argued case and present it to Government through constitutional channels. Possibly, if they had been intelligent enough to do so at that time, something constructive might have been achieved. Instead, the movement became more and more inclined towards subversive activities and violent demands, with the result that, before long, the then president, Mr. Harry Thuku, was arrested and held as a political detainee. This was in the very early days of the movement.

The arrest of Harry Thuku led his followers to stage an attempt to release him from custody whilst he was in Nairobi awaiting removal elsewhere to his place of detention, and there occurred what have been called the 'Harry Thuku' riots, during which some Kikuyu were shot and killed near the Nairobi Police lines where Harry Thuku was temporarily detained.

After these riots the K.C.A. was, for a time, driven underground, but it did not cease its activities, nor its agitation for the return of the land held by Europeans, in what had formerly been Kikuyu country.

The names of Jomo Kenyatta, Jesse Kariuki, and Joseph Kangetha now began to come into prominence as the new leaders of the movement, and there is little doubt that they regarded themselves as men with a mission; that they were fired with a burning desire to help their people and to set right the wrongs, both genuine and imaginary, that had been done to them. They continued to recruit members for the Association and, although for a time there was much less enthusiasm for a movement that was not approved of by Government and which, moreover, had led to the death of some of their comrades, the movement did not die out, but gradually gained strength.

Meanwhile, the leaders of the K.C.A. found that there were other matters troubling the Kikuyu besides the land question. They took these up and used them vigorously as a means of enlisting new members. They made great use, in particular, of the objection by some missionary societies to the Kikuyu custom of clitoridectomy, linked with the initiation of young girls from childhood to womanhood. For a variety of reasons which cannot be discussed here, but which I have discussed in detail in an earlier publication,[1] the operation on the female genitalia which was the 'outward and visible sign' for girls, which they received during the culminating stages of initiation into adult status, had become more and more severe, until the mutilation and resultant growth of scar-tissue was frequently causing grave trouble during childbirth.

The missionaries had also begun to be more fully aware of—and to oppose—the teaching that was given to the initiates. This, as we have seen, encouraged a certain amount of familiarity among the young men and women after initiation, although maintaining that full sexual intercourse, before marriage, was wrong.

Some of the missionary societies began to demand of their adherents that they should sign an undertaking, as a condition of remaining full members of the Church, that when their daughters reached the age of initiation they would not have them initiated. The majority of the Kikuyu took this to be a violent attack on an age-old custom which was considered essential to the welfare of the tribe, since, without initiation, girls could not become full members of the tribe, nor, by Kikuyu custom, were they eligible for marriage.

A wave of fury swept through Kikuyu country and the K.C.A. were not slow to take advantage of this in order to point out how greatly the white man, and particularly the missionary, was an enemy of the people. They said in effect, 'First the land has been taken from us' (forgetting to add that only a small part had been taken, and that in good faith), 'and now they attack our most sacred customs; what will they do next?'

The importance of this particular episode, from the point of view of our study of the causes of the Mau Mau, is that, more than anything else, it led to the start of many Kikuyu

[1] 'The Kikuyu Problem of the Initiation of Girls', in *J.R.A.I.*, 1931.

separatist churches and independent schools' organizations, both of which were closely affiliated to the K.C.A. political body and have been more recently the recruiting ground for hundreds of Mau Mau adherents.

For some time, a number of the Kikuyu adherents of the various Christian missions had begun to ask themselves whether the mission insistence on monogamy and on the abandonment of certain Kikuyu customs was really essential to the status of Christianity. The Swahili translation of the Old Testament, as well as almost the whole of the New Testament translated into Kikuyu, were by this time available for the people to read for themselves, and they could find no specific injunction against polygamy by Christ Himself (although they were assured that this was implied by certain passages). They found, rather, that it was a widespread custom in part of the Holy Book—the Old Testament—and they also found that many of their own 'heathen sacrifices' had counterparts in Hebrew custom.

Moreover, the word for circumcision used in the Bible (where, of course, it only applied to male circumcision) was translated in the Kikuyu version as *kurua*, a word which, for the Kikuyu, included the operation on the genitalia of both males and females and which provided the 'outward and visible sign' of initiation into adult status. Had not St. Paul said in so many words 'circumcision is nothing and uncircumcision is nothing'? Why, then, they argued, and on what authority, were the missionaries demanding the abandonment of female circumcision as a necessary qualification for full membership of the Church?

And so the movement to set up independent 'Christian' churches received impetus. There appeared the 'Kikuyu African Orthodox Church', the 'Kikuyu Independent Pentecostal Church' and a number of lesser religious movements, all with some degree of Christian doctrine, but with such modifications in teaching as the new priests and pastors and leaders of the movement saw fit to introduce.

From the outset, as we have seen, most of these independent churches were closely linked with the K.C.A. political
organization, and one of their main creeds was 'no interven-
tion from the white missionaries'. For the most part, at any
rate for a number of years, these independent churches used
the translations of the Bible provided by the missionary
societies, the Book of Common Prayer, and the mission
hymn books, but with such omissions as were considered
necessary.

The Kikuyu are by nature a very religious people, and,
for many who no longer had faith in the beliefs of their
fathers and who did not wish to subject themselves to some
of the stricter rules of conduct laid down by the established
missions, these new independent churches provided exactly
what they wanted—a means of religious expression and
communal worship which did not deter them from some of
their tribal customs that they wished to retain. The underlying teaching which these churches fostered, and which
was against the European missionaries, became, for many
of their adherents, a straightforward anti-white doctrine.

Closely linked with the two main separatist churches—
the Kikuyu Orthodox Church and the Kikuyu Independent
Pentecostal Church—came the foundation of the Kikuyu
Karinga Schools Association and the Kikuyu Independent
Schools Association, linked respectively with the Orthodox
and Pentecostal Churches. These school organizations,
which started mainly on the same basis as that of the
ordinary mission schools, have become more and more the
training ground for nationalist and anti-white sentiments.
It would be wrong to suggest that the schools have not done
a great deal of good in general education, and it may be
regarded as highly praiseworthy that these Kikuyu educational organizations financed and established a large
number of schools, making it possible for many children
who would otherwise still be illiterate to learn to read and
write. But these schools, like their parent churches, were

very closely linked with the K.C.A., which was all the time growing more and more violently anti-white, and openly subversive of established authority.

The fact that most of these independent schools rejected Government grants-in-aid, because the acceptance of such grants would involve their being subjected to inspection by education officers and conforming to a specific curriculum, emphasizes the anti-white trend. Recently Government has found it necessary to close many of the schools because it was discovered that they were closely connected with the spread of Mau Mau subversive teaching, and were even being used as centres for Mau Mau oath ceremonies.

When Peter Koinange founded the Kenya Teachers' College at Githunguri, in the Kiambu district, during the late nineteen-thirties, the object of the college was to train teachers, not only for the Kikuyu Karinga Schools Association and the Kikuyu Independent Schools Association, but also for schools to be started elsewhere among other East African tribes. The trainees were recruited mostly among the Kikuyu, but, from the outset, a proportion of young men from other tribes also went there to be trained as teachers.

The college was openly independent, but, in the beginning at any rate, it was not anti-white, and it supplied many much-needed teachers at a time when there was a great dearth of such men. Subsequently, Jomo Kenyatta, the former General Secretary of the K.C.A., became the principal of the college, which had always had the active support of the K.C.A., before that body was banned. This fact has certainly led many of the Kikuyu, with whom I have spoken, to believe that the college has latterly been used mainly as a training ground for politicians.

It must not be imagined, from what I have said so far, that all Kikuyu political developments have been anti-white.

When Harry Thuku, the founder of the original K.C.A.

in 1922, was released from detention he refused to return to the K.C.A. organization and started a separate political body known as the Kikuyu Provincial Association, which has throughout been very strongly opposed to the Mau Mau movement. The K.P.A., as it is called, is not unmindful of grievances among the Kikuyu people, but its methods are to try to persuade Government to bring in reforms through constitutional channels.

During the war years, the subversive activities of the K.C.A. led to the organization being banned, as well as to the detention of its leaders. When at length the leaders were released, the K.C.A., as such, was still banned, as was its official organ, the first Kikuyu newspaper, *Muiguithania*.

When the new political organization, known as the Kenya African Union, was formed in an attempt to weld together native opinion of many different tribes into a body that would have as its aim the improvement of conditions for Kenya Africans, former members of the K.C.A. were, as might have been expected, quick to rally to the new organization, and to seek in it means of continuing the activities of their own banned movement. By joining in large numbers they were soon able to control the appointment of its office-bearers, and so dominate this new political body.

Although no one would suggest that the K.C.A. of the past was synonymous with the K.A.U. of today, there is little doubt that, in Kikuyu country at least, most of the people leading the local branches of the K.A.U. are the same people who were formerly prominent in the councils of the K.C.A. Thus, to the masses of the Kikuyu within the Kikuyu lands, as well as to those on European farms, the K.A.U. became, to all intents and purposes, synonymous with the K.C.A., although any such connexion has been denied again and again through the administrative head-quarters of the K.A.U. organization in Nairobi.

When Jomo Kenyatta, the former Secretary-General of the banned K.C.A., became the President of the K.A.U., the widespread belief that the two organizations were one and the same became even stronger in the minds of the masses. Nor was this view lessened by the fact that many of its active leaders of branches of K.A.U., in other tribal areas, were people who had worked in close association with the K.C.A. before it was banned.

XI

THE GROWTH OF MAU MAU

It is not absolutely certain exactly when the Mau Mau movement started, nor yet how it came to get this name. I have not been able to find any meaning, or any reasonable explanation of the name, while most of the Kikuyu that I have asked say it is just a 'name without meaning'.

There is a certain amount of reason to believe that it was in the latter part of 1948 or early in 1949 that Mau Mau really got under way, and that this was linked with the news that the Duke of Gloucester was coming out to Kenya, as His Majesty's representative, to confer city status upon Nairobi.

It is certain that as soon as the news of this decision to grant city status to Nairobi was released, a number of Kikuyu agitators, most of them former members of the banned Kenya Central Association, started spreading the fantastic story that the raising of Nairobi to city status was to be accompanied by further 'thefts of land' from the Kikuyu by the British authorities. Since 'save the land' is the battle-cry that can stir a Kikuyu more than anything else, it was not surprising that a number of people, more particularly those who already felt a strong grievance about land matters, rallied to the call. Many meetings were held and people were called upon to boycott the city celebrations and everything to do with them.

It seems most unlikely that the leaders of this movement to boycott the city celebrations seriously believed that there was to be any further alienation of native land for European settlement, for they must have been fully aware that under the Natives' Land Trust Ordinance the lands that had formally been called 'Native Reserves' and which had once ranked as 'Crown Lands' were now fully safe-guarded.

However, the leaders of this movement were for some reason anxious to stir up further anti-British feeling, and they were fully aware that by saying that the land was in danger they were sure to get a following.

Certainly, at about that time and shortly before the Duke of Gloucester actually arrived, a big ceremony was performed in the Kiambu district at a place called Kiambaa, at which, according to many reasonably reliable accounts, a number of prominent Kikuyu took part in a solemn oath-taking ceremony, which included many, but probably not all, of the clauses of the oath ceremony that has more recently been shown to be associated with the Mau Mau.

That the persons who were organizing this movement would not stop short of violence, if they thought that their orders were being flouted, was shown by the fact that a Kikuyu member of the City Council, who not merely attended, but took a prominent part in the city celebrations, was shot at, though fortunately his assailants failed to kill him.

The vast majority of the Kikuyu regard the Mau Mau Association as nothing more than the old Kikuyu Central Association under another name. That this interpretation is correct seems to be supported by the fact that there is a remarkable similarity between the wording of the oath that was formerly taken by the K.C.A. (and which was one of the reasons that led to the banning of the Association) and the new Mau Mau oath. Moreover, the leaders of the old Kikuyu Central Association, who had been released from internment at the end of the war, tried in 1946 to revive the banned movement under the old name at the time when Jomo Kenyatta, the former General Secretary of the movement, came back to Kenya from England after a very long absence. This attempt failed and Government made it quite clear that the K.C.A., as such, would not be allowed to come back into existence. After this, for a time, the K.C.A. was never mentioned by Kikuyus either in speeches, or in the vernacular newspapers, but, under very thin disguise, the movement went on and was referred to as the 'Association of three initials' or, as the Kikuyu had it, the *Kiama Kia Ndemwa Ithatu*. If the authorities tried to suggest that the meetings of the 'Association of three initials' were illegal, on the grounds that it was, really, the banned organization, it was always possible for those taking part to reply that they were, in fact, referring to the three initials of some other political organization such as the Kenya African Union (K.A.U.) or the Kikuyu General Union (K.G.U.) which were bodies recognized by Government. They could thus avoid trouble, since it was almost impossible to prove that the 'Association of three initials' was the old K.C.A. and not one of the others.

If we accept the view that is widely held by loyal Kikuyu that Mau Mau is only another name for the old K.C.A. and for the later 'Association of three initials', we must not consider that all the former members of the K.C.A. became, automatically, members of Mau Mau. There were certainly some former K.C.A. members who had come to realize that the organization had done more harm than good to their cause, in its desire to get their land grievances settled, and who no longer gave their support to such movements.

At first, the Mau Mau movement was little heard of, and it probably only worked, in the early days, among people who were likely to approve of what was being planned. Obviously, it would have been most dangerous to approach really loyal Kikuyu and ask them to take the Mau Mau oath, for they would have refused and at once reported the movement to the authorities. Since, for the various reasons which we have examined, there were a great number of discontented Kikuyu among the squatters on European farms, the Mau Mau movement, from its probable start among a few leaders at Kiambu, was spread, first of all, in

97

the farming areas. But, even among the squatters, there were many who were loyal to the British and who were not willing to take the Mau Mau oath, and so, very soon, it became necessary to do a number of things that were contrary to native custom, if the movement were not to be discovered and stopped by the authorities before it became too strong.

It became necessary, in the first place, to force people to take the oath once they had been approached about it and had signified their unwillingness to participate on a voluntary basis. Unless such people were coerced into taking this oath, they would be a menace to the movement, but, if they could be frightened and forced into taking it, then the movement was safe.

This may sound very illogical to the English mind, for if one of us were forced to do such a thing, either by physical force or by threatening all sorts of reprisals to our family if we did not submit, or by actual acts of violence and torture, our first reaction, afterwards, would be to go and report the matter to the nearest police station. The leaders of the movement, however, knew the psychology of their fellow tribesmen so well that they felt reasonably safe in taking such action. We have already seen that a Kikuyu who takes a solemn oath is punished by supernatural powers if he breaks that oath, or if he has perjured himself. One of the phrases used in the Mau Mau oath ceremony is to the effect that 'if I do anything to give away this organization to the enemy, may I be killed by the oath'. Having once made such an oath, even under pressure, no ordinary Kikuyu would dare to go and make a report to the police or to his employer, because, were he to do so, he would be breaking the oath and thus calling down upon himself, or upon members of his family, supernatural penalties. But— the reader will argue—if a man had taken a Mau Mau oath against his will, why could he not then arrange for an immediate 'cleansing ceremony' and, having been cleansed and absolved from the effects of his oath, go and make a report to the authorities?

The answer to this question is really quite a simple one. While it is true that a person could be cleansed from the effects of a Mau Mau oath, participation in such a ceremony could not be kept quiet for long, since, to be effective, it must be carried out in public and before many witnesses. The Mau Mau people made it very clear to their victims that if they tried to get out of their obligations under the oath by such means, they would be victimized and even, if necessary, murdered.

From the Mau Mau point of view, therefore, the step that was taken of forcing people to take the oath against their will was a safe one, even though, by so doing, they were acting in a manner that was utterly and completely contrary to native law and custom, which has always laid down that an oath must be taken voluntarily and with the consent of members of the family of the person concerned.

It next became necessary to hold the oath-taking cere-monies at night, inside huts. This move was necessitated by the fact that, at this time, the movement was mainly being organized among squatters on European farms and there was always the likelihood that if an oath-taking cere-mony was organized by day, the owner of the farm might come along and want to know what was being done. More-over, if force were used at such a ceremony held in the open, in order to compel unwilling people to participate, there was the likelihood that some casual passer-by might hear the protests of the unwilling participants and report to the police or to the farmer that something was seriously wrong. This change-over to holding oath-taking ceremonies by night and inside huts instead of by day and in the open, also violated all the Kikuyu rules.

The leaders of the movement next decided to start administering the oath to women and even to children, as well as to adult males. It is not quite clear as to why this particular decision was taken, but, as we have seen, an oath taken by any member of a family was liable to bring supernatural punishment on any other member of that family. Clearly, if a woman could be persuaded, or forced, to take the Mau Mau oath, it would not bind her husband to the positive parts of the oath, i.e. it would not bind him to 'kill a white man when the war horn is blown', or to do such other positive acts, but it WOULD ACT IN A NEGATIVE MANNER, since it would prevent the husband from reporting on the ceremonies to the police. If he did so it would be tantamount to signing his wife's and his family's death warrant.

As an additional means of bringing pressure to bear upon fellow tribesmen to join the Mau Mau movement, the organizers called upon their members to have no dealings with people who had not joined. Mau Mau followers were forbidden to invite non-members to drink beer, or to attend their dances; they were not to help them in building huts or in any other tasks where it was normal for a man to call on his neighbours to give communal aid. Thus, many who had been reluctant to join the Mau Mau in its earlier days, were more easily persuaded to do so as time went on, especially in areas where the movement was strong.

The movement was so cleverly planned, in most respects, that it was able to grow rapidly, and there can be little doubt that had the leaders not overlooked two vital factors, the growth would have continued without attracting the serious attention of the authorities. Then when leaders felt that they had a large enough following they would have been able to act according to plan and start on a concentrated killing of 'the enemy, the white man'. Fortunately for the Europeans, for the many loyal Kikuyu, and for the country as a whole, the leaders had overlooked the fact that there were a proportion of Kikuyu who had so genuinely accepted the teachings of Christ that they had no fear at all of supernatural reprisals for breaking a heathen oath taken against their will. When the Mau Mau leaders, or rather their lieutenants in the districts, made the mistake of forcing such genuine Christians to take the oath, these people went as fast as they could and reported the matter to the police. Similarly a few old Kikuyu, who knew their ancient customs to the last detail, argued to themselves that an oath, taken under conditions which violated all the laws of oath-taking, was not a valid oath, and so some of them too, outraged at having been forced to act against their conscience, risked all and went and made reports.

Thus the authorities became aware of what was going on and prosecutions against those who had administered or had taken part in Mau Mau oath ceremonies began.

Another factor which made it impossible for the Mau Mau to remain the wholly secret organization which the leaders wished it to be (until the plans were ready), was that while the oath prohibited people who had taken it from 'telling the enemy', it did not, specifically, prevent them from talking about it to other Kikuyu who were among their friends. They certainly did not do this at all openly, nor did they explain all its details of the ceremonies to people who were not Mau Mau followers, but some of them did talk to their friends, and so gradually the masses of Kikuyu in the native land unit (who were still hardly affected by Mau Mau) got to know something of what was afoot. Gradually, too, quite a lot of information leaked out to the Kikuyu in general as to how the Mau Mau oath was administered, and many people were shocked.

Mau Mau ceremonies now began to take place on a much more extensive scale within the native land unit itself. Probably the leaders felt that too much was getting known about their plans. The police were already prosecuting cases that came to their notice in the settled areas, and the whole tempo of the movement was therefore speeded up. This was the only alternative open to the leaders other than abandoning the whole project, which they had no intention of doing. But it was much harder, in the overcrowded native lands, to hold Mau Mau ceremonies in secret, even at night, than it had been to do so among the squatters on the up-country farms. It therefore became more and more necessary, from the point of view of the leaders, to reinforce the fear of supernatural reprisals for breaking the oath, by threats of physical violence (and by actual violence) against any opponent of Mau Mau who dared report to the police. Thus started the era of arson and murder and the disappearance of witnesses who had been bold enough to make statements incriminating Mau Mau members to the police, or to the administrative officers. It was after this serious intimidation of persons who were against the Mau Mau began, that the opinion of the masses in the native land units—Nyeri, Fort Hall, and Kiambu—began to crystallize.

Up till that time, although more and more Kikuyu were aware, in a vague sort of way, that the Mau Mau movement was operating, and that people were being invited to join, or forced into taking the oath against their will, the people, as a whole, had not fully awakened to the dangers that were in their midst. When they did so, mass meetings were held denouncing Mau Mau and calling upon the people to resist it in every way possible. The first of these meetings took place in Nyeri district, where the worst cases of arson, designed to intimidate those who might have denounced the movement, had taken place. The Mau Mau leaders in the district got news that this meeting, to consolidate opinion against them, was to take place, and they staged a counter-ceremony, with a strangled and mutilated dog, in an attempt to scare people from the other meeting. But Mau Mau had to perform their ceremony at night, in the dark, and without public witnesses, and very few people therefore took it seriously. There followed similar meetings in Fort Hall and Kiambu, at which, in accordance with age-old customs, solemn oaths were taken against 'Mau Mau, enemy of the people'.

It was fully to be expected, and wholly in keeping with

known methods of the Mau Mau organization, that this action against them by large sections of the tribe should have resulted in greatly increased attempts to intimidate the masses, by murder and arson. The leaders probably hoped that the Kikuyu, as a whole, would be so terrified that they would be afraid to go further. Certainly the first murders had the effect of making more and more of the ordinary, loyal Kikuyus live in a state of terror. Nobody who was against the Mau Mau knew when there might not be a sudden invasion of his hut by armed men who would not hesitate to kill.

Clearly such a state of affairs could not be allowed to continue, nor could it be met by the ordinary processes of the law, which requires absolute proof, in accordance with our British rules of evidence, before a man can be punished by the courts. More particularly, it was impossible to continue to act by this slow method, when witnesses, who were willing to give evidence, kept 'disappearing', without a clue as to whether they had been murdered or merely persuaded, by violent threats against themselves and their families, to go into hiding and not give their evidence.

Thus it came about that the State of Emergency was declared, and none too soon. Suddenly the police, ably assisted by the armed forces, started to take really drastic action against the Mau Mau movement.

We have seen earlier in the chapter that, at the outset of the Mau Mau movement's activities, people who had taken the oath, under pressure, were afraid to undergo 'cleansing ceremonies' to rid themselves of the effects of the oath, because they knew that in order to be valid such action would have to take place in public, and there was the real risk that the moment they took such a step they would lay themselves open to reprisals.

Since the State of Emergency has been declared, more and more Mau Mau adherents have been asking for arrangements to be made for cleansing ceremonies, and this is a most heartening and welcome sign that Mau Mau power is felt, by the masses, to be on the downward trend. As I write this passage tonight, it has just been announced on the wireless that Mau Mau have staged a ceremony, involving the slaughter of a cat and a fowl, in the Nyeri area, as a warning of what people who do undergo the 'cleansing ceremony' may expect to happen to them and their families. This will probably not have any strong effect against such ceremonies, which may well be expected to go on faster and faster. It does, however, serve to show that it will be necessary for considerable protection to be given, for a long time, to the loyal Kikuyu and those who voluntarily renounce their Mau Mau allegiance.

With the declaration of the State of Emergency came the arrest of many of the most active leaders of the movement, and Mau Mau plans received a serious setback. But according to reports immediate steps were taken to appoint new leaders and lieutenants, and these people are continuing to administer the oath and are intensifying the drive for adherents to the cause. As resistance to taking the oath under pressure increases, people who have been enticed, or forced, to attend an oath-taking ceremony and who then refuse to submit to it, are being foully murdered. The dangers of the Mau Mau movement are still very grave indeed, and unless the new leaders can be identified and arrested, as they are appointed, an attempt may still be made to carry out the original intention of a wholesale attack on the European population.

XII

OUTLOOK FOR THE FUTURE

A great deal of publicity has been given to the suggestion that the Mau Mau movement 'is not the child of economic pressure or connected with any special grievances'.

It is true that Mau Mau, as such, is a terrorist organization whose principal aim is to drive the white man out of Kenya. I do not believe, however, that the movement could ever have achieved its present position if the genuine grievances which I have outlined in some of my chapters had not existed in the minds of a large part of the Kikuyu population.

It would be foolish to underrate the extent of the Kikuyu distrust of the European today; a distrust which has been cleverly fostered by Mau Mau leaders. It will be a long time before this attitude can be radically altered, but clearly, if some of the grievances are better understood and are removed, it will do much to alleviate the hostile attitude of the tribe. Otherwise, when Mau Mau has been suppressed, it will merely raise its head again under another name, at some future date. In this concluding chapter, therefore, I propose to discuss some of the things which can, perhaps, be done to improve the position.

I think I have made it clear that the biggest single grievance among the Kikuyu is linked with land. While the proportion of genuine Kikuyu land that was actually alienated for white settlement was very small in comparison with the whole tribal territory, Mau Mau and other political leaders have deliberately misled the present generation of Kikuyu into believing that the greater part of the White Highlands, the land occupied by European settlement, was also once Kikuyu land and was 'stolen' from them. This deliberate lie is fostered in order to make the

Kikuyu cast envious eyes on the whole of the land now occupied by European farmers. The greater part of the White Highlands, however, was never Kikuyu territory. It was land over which the pastoralist Masai grazed their cattle, and, in so far as it belonged to any tribe at the end of the last century, it belonged to the Masai. So far as I am aware, there is no evidence that the Masai ever claimed to own land on a family or individual basis, although different sections of the tribe had various special areas over which they roamed. In any event, those parts of Masai land which now comprise most of the White Highlands were transferred to European occupation on the basis of a treaty.

But if Mau Mau claims to almost the whole of the White Highlands on the allegation that it was formerly Kikuyu land are preposterous, the fact still remains that owing to increase of population, the Kikuyu land is today grossly over-populated. It is impossible for any but a few rich land-owners to earn more than a bare living from the land they occupy, whether as members of land-owning families, or as tenants.

The Kikuyu today are not content to live at a bare subsistence level. They want their children to go to school and this means paying fees and providing uniforms. They want to buy decent clothes for themselves and their families and the prices of these are very high. They want to buy a variety of foods which they cannot grow for themselves; tea, coffee, butter, wheat, flour, etc., as well as commodities like soap, mirrors, razors, gardening tools, and all the other many things which they have learned to use. In most cases, a family cannot hope to make enough money for these requirements from the sale of surplus produce from its small piece of land, as well as grow the basic food-stuffs of Kikuyu diet. Consequently there is practically no Kikuyu peasant family in the native land unit that has not got one or more of its members at work, away from home, supplementing the family income by working for a salary in the towns, cities, industrial concerns, or as employees on European farms.

This exodus from the native land unit is not, in itself, a bad thing. It means, however, that under present conditions a very large number of Kikuyu are leading dual lives. They are urban and yet not truly urban: they are peasant farmers occupying land in the native land units and yet forced to supplement their income by becoming partly urban. Very few Kikuyu earn large enough salaries, in their various forms of employment for the white man, to be able to give up this dual existence, and so become wholly urban. Similarly there are few Kikuyu families that can afford to be wholly peasant farmers.

The majority of the Kikuyu would much prefer to be wholly agriculturalists. They want sufficient land to be able to grow enough surplus crops to satisfy their various needs, as well as to grow their basic food supplies. Since this is impossible, at present, they are discontented and fall an easy prey to those who say 'Give us your support and we will give you all the land you need. We will drive out the white farmer and the land shall be yours.'

I believe, therefore, that additional land must somehow be found to satisfy this legitimate need of those who wish to remain agriculturalists. Is it possible to do this without inflicting hardship on others? I think it is. I believe there is still a good deal of land in Kenya which could be used for agricultural purposes, which is at present lying idle. It is land which has a reasonable rainfall and would grow good crops, but it has practically no permanent water. Permanent water is vital to peasant farmers, for they must have water when the dry season comes and they are harvesting their crops and preparing the land again for the following season. This water must be not only sufficient in quantity, but near to where they live.

Let it be said at once that a Native Land Settlement Board does exist and is studying this very problem of how to make some of this land available for further native settlement. The Board has been in existence for several years, but it has a great deal yet to do and I do not think it can ever achieve very much unless it is assured of very considerable financial backing. The water schemes that would be necessary, if any major contribution is to be made to the problem of resettlement, would be very costly indeed. But if there is a real desire to alleviate the terrible over-crowding of Kikuyu land, the money for such water schemes must be found.

I have referred to the fact that there are very many thousands of Kikuyu families living as forest squatters. Some method must be found to enable these people to go on working for the Forest Department and yet have a greater measure of security for the future. A labour force will always be needed by the Forest Department and, therefore, as the younger men in these families become more educated and more alive to the needs of better housing, some means will have to be found of making it possible to give them better homes. Security will also have to be provided for those who become too old to go on working, and who will not be able to go back and live in the native land units.

Then again there is the problem of the vast number of Kikuyu families who are squatters (who provide the 'resident' native labour) on European farms. The problem of these people is, in part, that of 'population increase' as I have already indicated, and, in part, due to the insecurity of their existence. From talks with hundreds of these squatters—in their own language—I know how their insecurity weighs upon them and causes much bitterness. I must admit that I do not know how this particular problem can be solved; yet a solution, acceptable both to the squatters and to the European farmers, will have to be found very soon.

Another thing that must be done in connexion with Kikuyu land problems and grievances, is to find a method

108

of meeting the desire of those who are land-owners to have a proper title to their land. If this were done, it would bring to an end, once and for all, the interminable litigation that goes on over land ownership, to which I have already briefly referred. Moreover, it would reveal what part of the overcrowded land is being occupied today by land-owners and what proportion of it by tenants, with little or no security. Unquestionably, it would be a very formidable and costly task, needing many surveyors, much patience, and untold wisdom, in order to ensure that false claims were not made by unscrupulous land grabbers, who would try to bolster up such claims by using bribery and corruption.

Whoever was in charge of this formidable task would have to be a man with such a detailed knowledge of Kikuyu law and custom concerning land tenure, that he could not be hoodwinked. Moreover, if this plan is to be effectively achieved, it would have to have the full support of the African leaders of all shades of opinion. Otherwise it would be deliberately made use of by agitators who would try to suggest that it was a trick of the white man to take away more land. I believe, however, that it can be done, provided that all Kikuyu leaders have it fully explained to them, in their own language, before anything definite is begun.

The next urgent problem that must be tackled is closely related to land and concerns the Kikuyu who are at present semi-urban, but who would like to become fully urban. It would only be possible for those who are at present semi-urban, with a house and a piece of land in the native land unit, to become fully urban if present-day conditions were considerably altered. It would be necessary for those who wished to become fully urban to earn sufficient salary to enable them to provide all the food that the whole of the family needed, together with all their other requirements in the form of clothes, school fees, European commodities such as soap, books, crockery, etc. In addition to earning enough to meet all these needs, they would have to be in a position to save enough money each month to be able to accumulate a fund for old age. But there is an aspect of this particular problem that is still more vital. If these semi-urban people are to become fully urban and cease to keep a footing in the native land units then a way must be found whereby they can come to own a home in the towns, instead of merely living in rented quarters.

As things are at present, very few employed Africans can look forward to a pension big enough to live on, or, in most cases, any pension at all, when their working days are done. Thus, it would be impossible for them to rent living quarters in the towns and cities on retirement. A man who had given up his place in the native land unit on becoming urbanized, would thus become homeless in his old age. Therefore, if it is considered desirable that the semi-urban people should become wholly urban, the present policy relating to native housing in the towns will have to be radically altered.

At present the city councils and municipal authorities build large African housing estates and rent cottages and rooms to Africans employed in the town—often at un-economic rates. Similarly, some of the big European commercial firms build quarters for their native staff, but these quarters are not owned by the Africans and are merely temporary homes. It will be necessary, I think, for the city and municipal authorities to continue to finance African housing schemes, but it would be better if the payments made by the African could rank as purchase instalments, instead of rent. By this means, during his working years, an urban African would gradually buy a house, and when the time came for him to retire he would have a home of his own. Since in all probability his family would be self-supporting by that time, he would then have a certain number of spare rooms in his house which he and his wife could let to young urban workers. From these rents, he would probably make enough money to keep himself and his wife. I am quite sure that unless some scheme along these lines is devised, it will continue to be impossible to create a truly urban native population, one which would relieve the present congestion in some of the native land units and especially Kikuyu land.

Another major problem in relation to Kikuyu land-hunger, that must be tackled fearlessly, is the problem of population increase. As I have already said, the Kikuyu formerly practised a form of birth control that was admirably suited to the conditions under which they lived in those days, but it was of such a nature that it is not capable of being applied today. The spread of medical facilities and the decrease in the death-rate, combined with the abandonment of birth control, is resulting in an increase in population which is economically impossible. Under present-day conditions of high cost of living and the need to educate children, a Kikuyu cannot really afford to have a very large family, especially since there are practically no free schools in Kenya. Most Europeans practise birth control and limit their families to the number they think they can afford. The Kikuyu today cannot do so, because they no longer have knowledge of the methods used by their forefathers which, in any case, are not suitable for modern conditions.

As far as I know, the British have done nothing constructive about setting up birth-control clinics for Africans, and meanwhile the rate of population increase is disturbing. It is, moreover, detrimental to the health of the mothers, to the training and feeding of the children, and to the economic structure of the family. Clearly something must be done to give the young Kikuyu knowledge of how to limit their families, and I believe this problem should be given a high priority.

This brings me to yet another urgent need, that of finding some way of reducing the heavy burden that the payment of 'marriage insurance' puts upon young Kikuyu men today, while it no longer provides the safeguards for marriage for which it was designed, the existence of which would be the only good reason for its retention. Already, there are a few Kikuyu families, perhaps one in ten thousand, which have taken the lead and have said in no uncertain terms, 'We will give up this custom, our sons will not pay marriage insurance, our daughters will be married without it.' Unfortunately this custom cannot be altered by the mere introduction of a law. Any attempt to force a change of this custom would be resented and would merely reinforce it. The only hope is to encourage the trend that has already started, at the same time educating the leaders in the wisdom of a change. If the acknowledged leaders of the people in religious, political, and social matters, were to abandon the present practice it would not be long before others followed suit. It is not so difficult as some people imagine for a custom to die a natural death, when the real leaders of the people have given a lead. In the last thirty years, the Kikuyu customs of piercing the ears, of knocking out the two lower central incisors of young people, and of the 'second birth' ceremony, have all practically ceased, although in 1920 nobody would have thought this possible. The leading people gave up these practices and so the masses followed.

I am sure that the answer to the problem created by the present break-down of the 'marriage insurance' system is to persuade those who are respected by the Kikuyu to abandon the custom. It will then die a natural death. I have addressed several African meetings on this subject in the past and I feel sure, from the reaction that I met with, that by persuasion and by careful explanation of the problems, this particular difficulty in Kikuyu life can be overcome.

I have referred at length to the fact that Kikuyu 'education', in its old form, was planned to train the young men and women for citizenship, so that they could take a proper, responsible position in adult society. I have mentioned, too, the lamentable failure of 'education' as it is given in the Kikuyu schools today to replace the character training of the old days. The Kikuyu demand for education at the present time is second only to their desire for more land and there is clearly a need for this demand to be met. More emphasis on technical training is necessary, but the need for a much greater stress on character-training is paramount. Unless the rising generation of Kikuyu (and of course this applies to other tribes as well) grows up with a better understanding of its responsibilities in a very complicated and exacting society, and of how to behave in such a society, there is little hope for the stable future we would all like to see; one in which all races in Kenya would work together for the common good.

I must now turn to the very difficult question of religion. The Kikuyu, as I have stressed—and must stress again—are by nature, religious. Agnosticism is not for them. They feel the need of a religion and many, in the past, have not been satisfied by the Christianity they have learnt from the various missions. I am quite sure that real Christianity is the answer, and by this I mean the teachings of Christ and not all the plethora of confusing doctrines and dogmas of the various churches that have so often been mistaken for fundamental Christianity.

In the olden days every Kikuyu was a complete and whole-hearted believer in the religion of his tribe; otherwise he could not be a full member of the tribe. It was hardly surprising, in the circumstances, that in the early days of the coming of the white man, the Kikuyu mistakenly believed that every Britisher was a practising Christian. When some of the British did things that no real Christian would have done, the Kikuyu was puzzled, and there is no doubt in my mind that the acts of some of the Europeans did a great deal to bring Christianity into disrepute.

A major challenge exists today for all Missions and all true Christians in East Africa; unless they can show that the teaching of Christ, rather than the various doctrines and dogmas of their respective churches, is the fundamental thing in their lives, and unless they can win the Africans back to a simple Christian faith, the pseudo-Christian teaching of many of the Separatist Churches will cause the gravest difficulties and provide fertile soil for subversive movements, movements which will be even more dangerous for the masses of Africans than for the white man.

Yet another problem to be tackled is the vexed problem of the colour-bar. There are many Africans in East Africa today, not a few of whom are Kikuyu, who are just as capable of proper behaviour in hotels and other places as most Europeans, and who are better mannered than some of these. It is virtually impossible, today, for an East African native, although he may have spent three years at Oxford or some other British university, where he suffered from no disability due to his skin colour, to have a meal in a public hotel or restaurant used by Europeans, even if he is accompanied by a European friend. This is a stupid attitude and one which is a source of much discontent. Clearly any hotel or other place should be able to reserve the right of admission, but the discrimination should not be on a basis of skin colour, but on behaviour. If a European wants to take an African friend to a meal in an hotel or restaurant, the onus should be on him to ensure that his guest behaves with decorum. If an African wants to go to such a place alone, then he must be able to show, by his behaviour, that he is a fit and proper person to do so. Clearly, no law can ever alter this position, but I do most seriously appeal to the Europeans of Kenya, among whom I count hundreds of friends, to give this matter earnest thought.

I think that I am aware of the arguments that the opponents of this idea put forward, but I am not convinced by them. I do seriously suggest that the good will that would be gained by a reasonable approach to this problem would be so very worth while for the future of our country that it must be given a fair trial.

Linked with this is the question of differential rates of pay, based upon colour and race and not on ability. A more rational approach to this problem is urgently needed. Salary scales should depend on ability and upon nothing else. Some of the most embittered leaders of anti-white propaganda are those who have university degrees and who never had any of their fees reduced on account of the colour of their skin, but who found, on returning to Kenya, that no matter what their qualifications, their colour and race precluded them from earning salaries even comparable to those of Europeans with lesser qualifications.

To bring this book to an end, I must briefly discuss language. Many of the difficulties of the present time are greatly increased by the fact that few Europeans can speak Kikuyu idiomatically and accurately. Although an ever-increasing number of Kikuyu are learning English, it is still necessary for Europeans to make use of Kiswahili when talking to Kikuyu. Kiswahili is not the language of the Kikuyu or the European, and it fails lamentably as a medium of real understanding between ourselves and the average Kikuyu.

Since most Europeans are very bad at learning an African language, and since Kikuyu is a very difficult language to learn, I feel that the teaching of English must be speeded up, in order that there may be a better understanding of our policy, our laws, and our teaching. Let anyone who doubts the wisdom of this idea try to imagine the chaos that would result if a German tried to convey his ideas to the average Englishman using the French language as his medium.

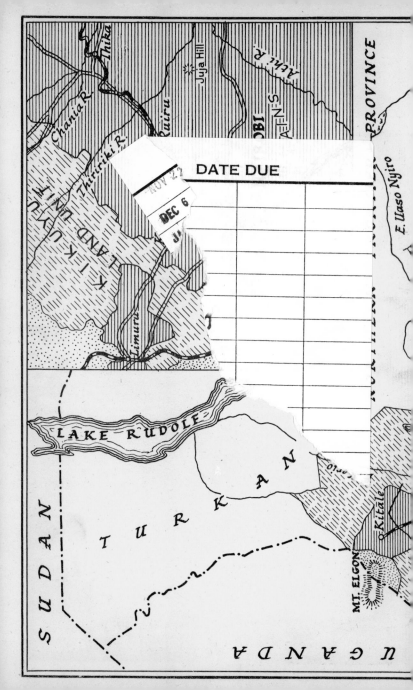